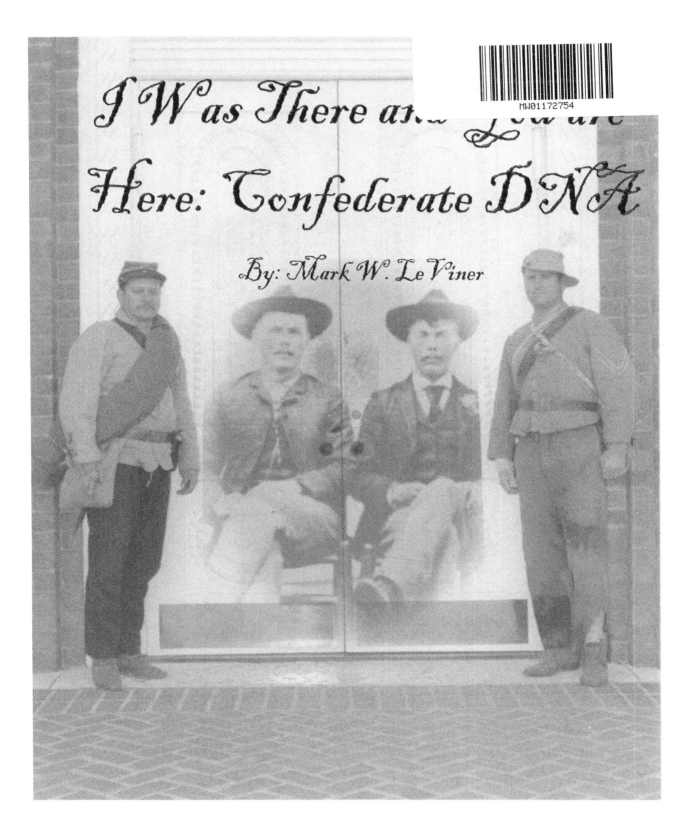

I Was There and You are Here: Confederate DNA

By: Mark W. Le Viner

05/17/2014

Written by Mark Leviner Edited by Lynell Leviner

On the Cover: left to right Mark Leviner, Elisha Dowless, Samuel Dowless, Judson Leviner. Brothers are flanking brothers. Samuel is the great-great grandfather of Mark and Judson. Elisha and Samuel served in the 36th N.C. 2nd Company I of Heavy Artillery. Both fought at Ft. Fisher, N.C.; were captured and then imprisoned at Pt. Lookout, Maryland; released in June of 1865. We are posed in front of the Lee Chapel at Lexington, Va. The photo work by Paul Collins combines an 1862 photo with one from the year 2000.

Table of Contents

Acknowledgements   page 5

Introduction   page 7

Chapter 1...1993-2006   page 14

Chapter 2...2007   page 47

Chapter 3...2008   page 62

Chapter 4...2009   page 83

Chapter 5...2010   page 100

Chapter 6...2011   page 139

Chapter 7...2012   page 165

Chapter 8...2013   page 199

Chapter 9...2014   page 234

Chapter 10...2015   page 270

Afterword   page 298

Acknowledgements

Special Thanks to reenactors of the South and North. This definitely includes those of the 51st Virginia, 28th Virginia, and 1st Kentucky. Thanks for all of the wonderful memories. I will never forget you all.

Pat Owen, John, and Michael Leviner gave assistance with technology as did Byron Jones who did family tree research as well. Louise Jones and Margie Jones saved my wife and me with major help when we were ready to have a meltdown with the computer program. Thank you all so much!

Thank you, Paul Collins, for taking some amazing pictures that I included in this book. I appreciate Michael R. Bradley for writing a beautiful poem that I included in this book, "I am Their Flag," and thanks to H. K. Edgerton for touching my heart with his delivery of it. It always gave me chills and brought tears to my eyes.

Tom Perry gave advice and assistance with publishing. Thank you so much for all of your help. Mr. Perry has written or published over fifty books.

Thank You Robert Brown for the gift of the Journal I would use to record more in detail the 150th Anniversary Events. And Thanks for the interest in reading what I wrote and your kind support. Oh yeah and being brave enough to take the picture on page four.

I guess I would be remiss if I did not thank my older brother, Eddie, who wrote another poem I included, "One Wore Blue, the Other Wore Grey." Also, thanks to my mom, Doris Ward Leviner Smith, for all of the stories she read to me. Her Maiden name of Ward is also my middle name. Now I have a story for ya'll to read.

Introduction

I Was There, and You are Here

Confederate DNA

Hello, come along and journey with me, I will tell you of a few of the times I spent in a Confederate uniform. Because of the miracle of DNA there can be no denying our real identities or where we come from, but we get to choose where we are going, just as they did. Every human is on a journey. Every life is a gift from God. I choose to not forget the sacrifice of men and women of the South who gave the gift of their lives toward a cause of love for limited government, the government of their Revolutionary War forefathers. Their war was a terrible one, their deaths many, their wounds deep. The war was fought over divisions of thoughts on subjects like money, commerce, politics, and slavery. Not everyone in the South fought for slavery or everyone in the North fought to free slaves. The word Confederate does not mean slavery. It is a bringing together word. The Southern States were together and yet each one was recognized as its own entity. As humans we share this world and yet no two of us are alike. This book has an alternative motive, it is to bring you and me closer together yet give you respect because you are purposely and wonderfully made. Remember the southerners who fought in 1861-1865 were Americans too. I will address the slavery issue more later to include my slave ancestor and black slave owners.

My name is Mark LeViner, and I was a Confederate reenactor from November, 1993, until April, 2015. My life has been greatly enriched by the people I met and the knowledge I gained. My DNA, present all the time, I will not discover though until my reenacting days are over. My interest in the Confederacy came early in life. At the age of six, my dad took my older brother Eddie and me to a Centennial Parade in Danville, Virginia. This was at the last Capitol of the Confederacy, the Sutherlin mansion. I had been born in 1959 only two-tenths of a mile away. The reenactors in the parade were solemn in appearance and their uniforms made an impression. Often as a lad I marched with imaginary soldiers at my side. A gray jacket was my uniform and a tall stick my rifle. From 1970 to 1976 we lived at a place called Mt. Holly, North Carolina. I witnessed firing of black powder guns here. A club would gather to shoot on the empty grounds of the Jr. High School over the hill. One hand would be at the trigger housing and the other on the butt stock or plate, to keep their shoulders from getting sore. My best friend Stuart Bailey had a real "civil war" bayonet with about 2 inches of the tip broke off. We enjoyed throwing it around. I heard a pile of them was buried nearby so I begged off on mom and dad to get me a metal detector for Christmas. I never found the bayonets. Sometime later, my big brother would write a poem entitled "One Wore Blue, the Other Wore Grey":

Can you give me a moment

Of your memory and mind,

To look back on an age

That was priceless in time?

When boys were dressed

And sent on their way,

One wore blue

The other wore grey.

They carried two flags

Of colors and stars,

One waved stripes,

The other waved bars.

As each left home

The families would pray,

For the boys in blue

And the boys in grey.

The prayers were heard

By a God who cared,

But in the sorrow to come

they all would share.

The Heavens gave no answer,

The sky had no say

For one day it was blue

And the next it was grey.

So, they picked up guns

And to war they did go,

For love of country

Their blood would flow.

As the battles went on

Men died by the way,

Some wore blue

And others wore grey.

After four years of fighting

The glory was gone,

Tired, weary men

Just wanted to go home.

But some had their rest

In the graves they lay,

Hands folded on blue

Hands folded on grey.

As fate would have it

The North did win,

For the South would break

Before she could bend.

As the two men met

Shook hands and rode away,

One wore blue

The other wore grey.

What more can I say

About this feeling inside,

When I think of the men

Who left me heritage and pride?

Pride that brings a tear to my eye

As I remember that glorious day,

When men wore blue

And men wore grey.

Eddie LeViner

Years later as a reenactor, more memories would be made at this place in Danville, Virginia. The youngest of my three brothers also born in Danville is Joseph Judson LeViner. In the month of January for seven straight years, we would join in a parade marching up to the last Capitol in efforts to support the flying of the Third National Flag of the Confederacy, its last National Flag. Of all the places in the world it should be allowed to fly, it should here as a memorial and as part of the Nation's history. We were always in our Confederate uniforms and always carrying our 3 band Enfield rifles. Volleys were fired in honor and tribute. Later on, I was at a 'Civil War Roundtable' meeting and met a man who remembered me from the parades. He gave me a map showing two sites of buried Confederate treasure in Danville. He had tried legal means to obtain it and failed. I am happy for it to stay where it is as Jefferson Davis, the South's President, would have wanted it to stay, and besides, I guess the government would get it anyhow. I would also be a guard at the Sutherlin mansion during reenacting of the last Cabinet meeting which was held here.

After my time of reenacting, there is another memory I wish to relate. By some trickery, the Third National Flag of the Confederacy we had earlier gotten to fly on a piece of ground of the United Daughters of the Confederacy (UDC) on the grounds of the Sutherlin

mansion was taken down. Soon after, very large Confederate Navel Jack Flags begin to appear on private property around Danville. A group called the Virginia Flaggers offered assistance. Sometimes on my job, I would come around by Danville driving a big rig from Martinsville to Tidewater, Virginia. I would always like it when two drivers would let me tag along. They were Roger Mitchell and Henry Hodges. Henry is a friend to the Virginia Flaggers.

Let's see the Confederate Battle Flag for what it is. It is a Christian Flag. In the battle of First Manassas, or First Bull Run, there was much confusion on both sides caused by uniform colors and flag designs being similar. The Confederate battle flag was designed by William P. Miles and adapted by General PGT Beauregard as the battle flag of the Army of Northern Virginia. Carried into battle by Trinity believing Christians, the flag was intended to put the fear of God into the hearts of the Yankees. An example of a northerner who was not a Trinity believing Christian was Julia Ward Howe who wrote the "Battle Hymn of the Republic." The red field represents the Blood of Christ. The White border represents the Protection of God. The Blue X represents the Christian Cross of

Saint Andrew, the first Disciple of Christ Jesus and patron Saint of Scotland and Russia. The thirteen stars represent the Southern States of Secession. According to the booklet The Confederate Book of Arguments by John D. Long, the message in the Confederate Battle Flag is: "Through the Blood of Christ, with the protection of God, We, the Thirteen States, United in our Christian fight for Liberty". You can plainly see how this flag is for every race because Jesus died and rose again so all could be saved if they would. Some of every tribe and nation will be in Heaven. The X is in the flag of Scotland where many Southern soldiers could trace their ancestry back to. A portion of my ancestry is found there also. Another name for the Confederate battle flag is the Southern Cross.

In the pamphlet The Truth About the Confederate Battle Flag by John Weaver, it states that Andrew, the disciple of Christ, requested a cross of this shape for he felt unworthy to be crucified on a cross as was Christ. He was crucified three days. He preached to everyone who came by. Finally, so many people were impressed by his preaching that they requested him be taken down. When he was, he fell dead, a martyr for Jesus Christ.

CHAPTER 1...1993-2006

It is in early November of 1993 that I bum a ride with my youngest brother, known in reenacting circles as Jud. Thanks to him for taking the plunge before me and helping me with equipment and clothing to get me started. From Stuart, Virginia, to Eastern North Carolina we arrive on Friday night. The weather is mild for this time of the year, and we join others to sleep under the tall Carolina pines. This place is known as Ft. Branch. The actual fort is earthen and on a tall bluff of the Roanoke River. This event is a place of great tactical or unscripted battles. These may lead off through an area swamp and end up in one of the many cotton fields. It turns out that brother Jud and I lay in heavy brush to ambush the pursuing Yank. We fire off two loads of black powder to let the good- natured Billy know we got the drop on him. Here I was at the age of 34 thinking how old I was. When looking back, I realize our great-great grandfather was 35 when he volunteered to serve in the Confederacy. This place holds me in its charm and will always be one of my favorite places on earth.

As I recollect, our next event is at the battle of Bentonville, N.C., in March of 1994. This is my first battle fighting with my new Unit, the 28th Va. Infantry. I am so excited that I forget my shell jacket. Upon arrival, Tom Ward is kind enough to loan me one. We have a Company meeting here and Dave Cornett is promoted to Captain now. This also bumps up Greg Gallion and Dave Lawhorn in the ranks. Dave Lawhorn gives me good advice. He says to mentally dress yourself before you leave for an event seeing that you have each article. The first picture of my reenacting career is taken here. I wear the borrowed coat as Jud and I stand ready for a blanket inspection.

At this time, I am setting about to grow a beard. It should be noted that I have not started keeping a journal yet and have not had an idea for writing a book. Event passes I have saved now bear witness to these Events I attended even though my memory has faded.

4TH
ANNUAL

STUART
BIRTHPLACE
ENCAMPMENT

1994

The above-mentioned Carolina Campaign is March 18 and 19, we will not stay for Sunday. This is often the case over the next several years as often on Sundays I teach Sunday School. I will come to fight on Sundays later, reasoning how 'Stonewall' Jackson himself did, but he did prefer not to.

At the Wilderness Campaign of May 6 and 7, I buy a cartridge box as best as I can remember. Gettysburg, the second day, comes up July 1 and 2, 1994. This is a big event and big events mean more Sutlers to shop at. This is where I buy my second black slouch hat, the first being at Ft. Branch. This second one will stick with me. I need to have a hat that looks similar to the one my Confederate ancestor is wearing in what may be the only photo ever taken of him. At the end of a reenacting day, the 28th Va. goes to the Virginia monument at the

Gettysburg battlefield to get our picture taken, the route of 'Pickett's charge' lays before us. We are all in our Confederate uniforms but are not allowed to carry our rifles as we retrace the steps of the original 28th in the charge as they did 131 years before. We are in two ranks and carry our flag. Ed Lee is our flag bearer. His given name is Robert E. Lee. It is said his ancestor, John Abbot Independence Lee, was the first man in Pickett's Division over the wall. It is told that he waved the battle flag of the 28th Virginia before being shot twice and captured. We cross the Emmitsburg Road and lean forward a bit as one would being under heavy fire by an entrenched enemy. Once over the wall, we gather and sit. 1st Lt. Gallion starts our memorial service with a prayer where we cry more now. Our Captain Cornett reads aloud a description of the 28th's involvement in the charge having to stop and compose himself so that he might go on. The original Captain of the 28th saw his son mortally wounded and gave him water from his canteen before leading the men on to the wall. His son was a drummer boy. We have two drummer boys here with their dads: Joshua and his Dad Larry Van Deventer, and Chris with his Dad Al Henry. Al plays "Amazing Grace" on the fife being joined by the drummers. Sergeant Lawhorn gets his voice back for a defiant yell.

On July 16, 1994, these words were penned from Knollwood Troutville, Virginia:

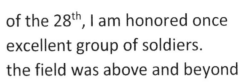

"Gallant men again to have led an You're conduct on of the 28th, I am honored once excellent group of soldiers. the field was above and beyond the call of duty! Anytime fighting is to be done the 28th can be counted on. All of us were touched I am sure, by the service done at the wall. I am honored to have had a part and the experience as I am sure many of you are too. This was an experience that we can carry with us all our lives. Let us all remember the Craig Mountain Boys and do them honor in all we do. God bless each and all and I'll see you in Salem."

Capt. Dave Cornett 28th Virginia, Company C Commanding.

On July 30-31, the 3rd annual battle of South Salem is held at Green Hill Park. It is sponsored by Roanoke County Parks & Recreation and is another of the 'Civil War' reenactments held in Virginia.

The 130th 'Battle for Lynchburg" is held Sept. 16th, 1994, for us at least, at Forrest, Virginia. In October 1994, we attend the 130th Anniversary of the "Battle of Cedar Creek". Let us hear from the Captain once again:

"Gallant men of the 28th,

It is difficult to believe a reenactment season is coming to a close. It seems only a short time ago the 28th Va. was only a dream! You have honored yourselves above and beyond what your Captain thought possible! From the gallant stand against the Yankee invaders on our front and rear at Bentonville, to the rout of the Yankees at the Wilderness; where you captured 4 artillery units and two stands of Colors and received a corps commendation; to the honor paid to our ancestors at the wall at Gettysburg; to the disciplined order in which you pressed the vile Yankees at Lynchburg earning the subsequent of 'shock troops'; to the gallant way you refused the flank at Cedar Creek while protecting the left flank of the corps.

You men have advanced yourselves a long way in a short time, and indeed, with the honor you have rendered unto our ancestors; you men have earned the right and privilege to call yourselves soldiers of the 28th Virginia! It has been my extreme pleasure and honor to have served as your commander thus far and I must say, that with fighting men as dedicated as yourselves to such a noble cause, the sentiments of General Armistead come to mind: 'You know the gravity of the situation and would do it without an officer to lead you'. With such gallant men as this, it is indeed easy to be a commanding officer. Each of you is to be commended for an excellent season of work! I look forward to serving with each and every one of you in campaigns to come! I remain,

Your obedient servant,

Capt. Dave Cornett,

Commanding 28th Va. Co. C.

May God bless each and every one of you and yours!"

Knollwood October 28, 1994

I do not have all the passes from all the events I attended, but for some reason not known to me, I kept count of every one of these Reenactments.

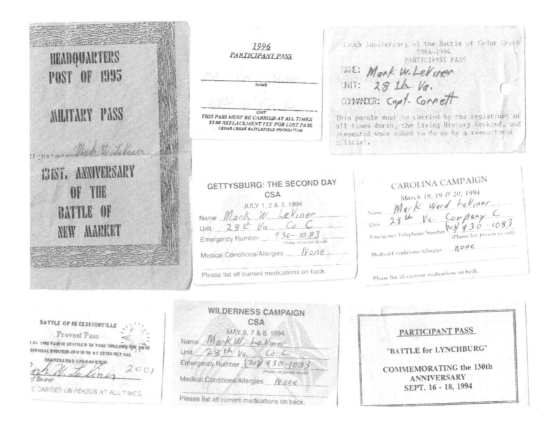

In January, 1995, the wife and kids are along with me to view the Atlantic Ocean here at Ft. Fisher, North Carolina. This is the 130th Anniversary of this battle. When and if a reenactor goes to a battle their ancestor was in, it becomes

a special event. I am in a night battle which is rare in itself. As I fire into the advancing Yanks on the high earthen mounds, my rifle main spring breaks. That is what can happen when shortcuts are taken, like boring the musket nipple bigger, thinking it will not clog and be easier to clean. Undeterred, I am shy no longer as I go to talking to the spectators in line, telling them about my ancestor who fought here. These lines I wrote, I share with you:

I WAS THERE AND YOU ARE HERE

Four generations ago, a hundred years or so,

Samuel A. Dowless was born in 'Civil War' his country was torn.

At Fort Fisher, North Carolina he was to be.

The first routing of U.S. Marines he was to see

A most heavy bombardment he was to survive

In hand to hand combat heroes would strive.

The need of States Rights still very clear

For I was there and he is here.

One hundred thirty years ago to this day

He wrote a letter before he was sent on his way.

To his wife and children it went,

For their good it was meant.

'God is with me' he would write.

Five months at Pt. Lookout, Maryland was his plight,

Thirteen children he and his wife finally had.

They stuck together through good and bad.

So is one generation two more would appear

I unborn was there, and he dead is yet here.

One hundred thirty years later, me my brother

and comrades came to the old fort,

like you, your brother, and comrades, to the yanks

our muskets gave a sharp report.

Although none died, we did remember ya'll men,

the old south and the way things were back then.

Ahead in time my mind wanders.

Inside the Pearly Gates it ponders

As he looks over my shoulder he says, 'I was there'

and as his eyes meet mine, he exclaims

and now you are finally here.

January 17, 1995

April the first finds Jud and I attending a living history at the last Capitol of the Confederacy in Danville, Virginia as I have referenced earlier, which also the last Cabinet meeting is reenacted.

May of 1995 finds us marking the 131st Anniversary of the "Battle of New Market." In October of 1995, as we are marching at 'Shoulder Arms', a picture is taken. From this picture a painting is done using many of us as models. Prints are made of which one hangs on my living room to this day. Brother Judson and I are at a 'J.E.B. Stuart event in 1995 as well. The early ones were held in June.

'The Battle of Lee's Mill' at Endview is in March 23 of 1996. We are allowed to use ramrods and have fixed bayonets, for this grand opening. In 1996, I was in my Confederate States Marine Corps uniform when I joined many other reenactors in a march down Monument Avenue in Richmond, Virginia. We were part of the Centennial Celebration of the Sons of Confederate Veterans.

In July of 1996, I go to the battle of Gettysburg, held at Fairfield not far from actual Gettysburg, Pennsylvania. I only have fifteen dollars for the weekend. Judson lets me ride with him and we make good use of the dog tent. I have my big clunky cam recorder to tape the event. We go to the actual battlefield and I record scenes as I did in the town as well as in the town of Fairfield. We are a long way from home and stay over on Sunday. I am granted special permission and am imbedded with the 28th Va. Infantry. I film before and during the battle. I catch some embarrassing moments in weapons inspection, men cheering and jeering, tremendous cannonading, and then into battle. I have my 9-button sack coat off to try to hide the camcorder. I record volleys, attacks up the hill, and sprawling 'hits. The fellows know that I am recording and put the effort in for a realistic looking fight. Many VHS copies are made, and, in later years, there are DVDs made.

On the last day of 1996, I take my sons John age 10 and Michael age 8, and my 3-band Enfield rifle to deer hunt. We arrive on site in my 1984 Monte Carlo Super Sport two door car. Michael gets out of the front seat; John is sitting in the back seat, barefoot. I tell him not to touch the rifle butt at his feet. He draws up his feet and doesn't touch the rifle. It is overcast and rain is expected, not much daylight. This picture is of an upside down 35mm negative, the Drs. Assistance took. I traded him a bullet for pictures. This is the exit wound.

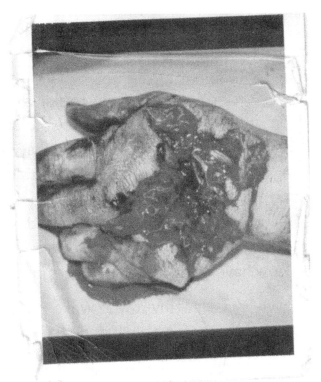

'Haste makes waste' is a statement of great truth. In my left hand, I reach to get my hunting knife and 3-inch brim camo soft hat. My right hand reaches for the long barrel gun. I catch it on top of the barrel as I expect to drag it out of the car further so as to put my hand then under the barrel to carry it. As I pull the gun, it goes off, caused by static electricity. At point blank range, the 90 grains of FFF black powder propels the 560-grain weight conical-shaped hollow point bullet through the palm of my right hand, knocking it back as far as it would go around by my back. I think to myself that it just knocked my hand off the barrel as it didn't even hurt. When the hand starts back around, the back of it catches my eye, the exit wound side. I know this mistake cannot be hidden. I am a broken man. It is at this precise moment that God does a work in my life. He gives me everything I will need to live with this the rest of my life and it does not include pity. A great love comes over me and it is for you, whoever you are. I know it is not all about my hand; even though as I'm told later, I have arterial bleeding, I do not fear I will die from this. I hold my hand

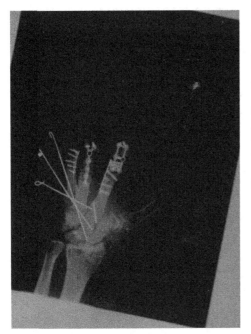

to my chest and walk down to the road for help, after knocking on the door where I used to live. No one is home as I knock but soon the preacher who lives there now arrives to put a tourniquet on my arm. It will take 10 surgeries to make my hand useable. I think of the soldiers of the 1860's, it would have been one surgery, amputation.

Two years to the very day, I go back in the same car to park and go deer hunting with the same rifle, this time alone to take care of business. Up on a mountainside in the snow, I walk on a blown-over tree to pull down on a deer between two trees in the forest. The herd moves on this one slowly. My second shot finds its mark also passing completely through the deer, just like with other deer I have hunted in the past. I will stop using the rifle to deer hunt and use it only for reenacting now. I hear it may be a possibility of some lead residue left in the barrel, although the rifles are inspected very closely at events, so I find it hard to believe. With this rifle I now have blood sweat and tears invested.

While in a lengthy stay at Wake Forest Baptist Hospital in Winston Salem, North Carolina, I receive a painted-on canvas framed Battle flag of the 28th Va. Infantry. On the back is a message with 21 signatures. The message is:

"Brother Mark,

We are humbled to have a compatriot such as you. We want you to know that the hurt you feel. We feel too! We are here for you as well as with you. We would want you to know that our thoughts and prayers are constantly with you and your family.

Your Brothers in Arms,

Captain Cornett, Lt. Greg Gallion, 1st Sgt. David Lawhorn, 2nd Sgt. Jerry Aldhizer, Sgt. Pete Camper, 1st Corp. Larry Van Deventer, Cpl. Ed Lee, Cpl. Judson LeViner and Privates Dan Baker, Jeff Bower, Doug Camper, Jim Day, Keith Hedrick, Leland Hedrick, Robbie Lawrence, Mark Musick, Bill Saunders, Bill Sieser, Jeff Sobataka, Donald Whitacre, and Jim Wood.

At my next event back after the accident, I am offered the job of Sgt. Major, I'm sure due to my hand. I turn it down and now try to learn to use my hand the best I can at my favorite rank, private. This is at Newbern in Pulaski County, Virginia, in July of 1997. This is an event we attend more than once. On one occasion here, my brother Judson loses his rifle or has it stolen. He lays it down to help put up tents. It may be an outsider who takes it. In my experience, reenactors as a whole are honest, trustworthy folks. The Company provides Jud with a replacement. First Sgt. Dave Lawhorn has used it and his initials are carved on it, DWL. He says, 'This also stands for Down with Lincoln."

In another memory of this place, we are in a heated battle and it is not going well for us. One of my sons is our flag bearer when Jim Wood comes to the rescue. He takes our Confederate battle flag and flees the pursuing Yankee

Cavalry. He plunges into a briar patch where they dare not to go. Jim is our sole survivor, and our flag does not fall into the hands of the enemy!

In the early fall of 1997, I take the kids to Maryland to the 135th Anniversary battle of Antietam or, as Confederates say, Sharpsburg. One time Jud and I explored the town before going to the famous Burnside's Bridge. At this event, we actually get paid. Professional photographer and 28th Va. soldier, Paul Collins, takes our picture. The company poses at the cornfield as well. It will later be flattened in the battle there.

Photos by Paul Collins

Photo by Paul Collins

The first of November, I return to Ft. Branch, North Carolina. In April of 1998, I am at the 133rd Anniversary of the battle of Sayler's Creek, Virginia. I attended this event several times over the years.

 It was here in 1993 that I bought the rifle I still have. It is a 3-band reproduction Armi Sport 58 cal. 1853 Enfield made in Italy. It was an extra from a movie set and feels lighter than your average rifle.

I also am here in 1993 with my two sons and brother Judson visiting when I videotape Bob Moates portraying General Lee. He is telling about the battle and looks the most like the General than any other I would ever see. Memories flood in from times spent here.

The time we wade the actual creek and, at least, get to take off the brogans first. Jerry Aldhizer captures a Yankee banner and refuses to give it up. I see him being carried off behind the Hillsman House surrounded by the Federals, his feet not touching the ground. It is also here that my youngest son, Michael, takes his first 'shot' in a reenactment. The Yankee he 'shoots' actually falls, a rare occurrence. General Hillsman, whose ancestors lived in the house on the battlefield, is the first Commander of Longstreet Corps of which the 28th Va. Infantry is a part of. I remember him having cancer and still being at this event. We miss him dearly.

May the 29-30, 1998 is 'The Clark House Battle' in West Virginia. It is hosted by The Order of the Bonnie Blue and the newly formed 'Flat Top Copperheads' Sons of Confederate Veterans Camp. It is held in Pipestem Park. I believe this the event where 'Rap a Dan' Dan Baker of the 28th Va. is 'shot' with black powder as he turns a corner of the old cabin. His belly is quite red from the close quarters shot as I recall.

 I reenact in more than one location in West Virginia in the early years. Once we are near a school but no students about as it is a weekend.

At this event, I am employed as a scout, a job that is dangerous and exciting. A huge log is used in the building of a shebang or crude shelter here. These shelters comprised of materials at hand could turn up at any event. Others may just curl up on a ground cloth in a blanket to spend the night. I find this works best when a fire is close by.

In June, I make my only pilgrimage to Point Lookout, Maryland. This is the site of the large prison camp where my ancestor Samuel A. Dowless and his brother Elishia were sent after their capture at Ft. Fisher, North Carolina. I am touched by this visit and jot down the following words before I leave, having brought my sons along, too. It's dated June 13, 1998 and addressed to Samuel A. Dowless: The old cabin still stands in Bladen Co. North Carolina.

"You came to Pt. Lookout from the Tarheel State. Me, from across the line, the town of the last capital of the Confederacy. You came here 133 years ago from your home via Ft. Fisher. Me, 133 years later via Richmond. I didn't know the horrors of Ft. Fisher. But I do know what it's like to be shot with a Musket. I don't know what it's like to be a 38-year-old prisoner at Pt. Lookout. But I know what it's like to be a 39-year-old visitor. Here at Pt. Lookout last night, I couldn't sleep at all. You were always on my mind. For after all you spent five months of misery day and night here. Today I stood where you stood, walked where you walked. We honor you and your comrades today and the grove where thousands of them lay. Last year I visited your home, the old cabin still stands. The grave is well marked and kept up, your dear wife still by your side. I don't know when we can talk, but I know we will, for I do know your God."

Mark LeViner.

Welcome to the 135th Anniversary Battle of Gettysburg.

This is the largest reenactment of the whole war, and I thought it might only be topped by the 150th, but it was not. For events such as this, I take a day or two off from work. I take my family also so they can experience one of those "events of a lifetime." On the way up to Pennsylvania, we stop off in Harper's Ferry, West Virginia. We have a lunch here of food we bring called MRE's or Meal's Ready to Eat. One of the saddest things I recall seeing is upon arrival. Brother Judson has a new bride, Melody, and she is stopped when trying to get to the camp, a line of soldiers would not let her pass through their line. She and Judson had quite a fine period wedding. They had passed under the crossed rifles of the 28th Va. members so designated at their wedding.

Our camp is in some woods, I have to park in a field a far off. On the first morning, I hear a yell as some sleeping in some leaves are nearly run over. The Porta-Johns I see earlier have been moved away from us, so we have to create a place to go. We are joined at this event by some foreign reenactors as is often will be the case at large well-known battles. On the last day of Gettysburg in Pickett's Charge, the Battle Flag of the 28th Va. Infantry was captured by the 1st Minnesota at the original battle. The Minnesotans are here, and the plan is we will reenact this. There is no help from the higher uppers, so we must pull it off. We field 45 troops in the 28th Va. Co. C Craig Mountain Boys, some of the overseas fellows are in with us. The 1st Minnesota has been beefed up with an Indiana unit. There are at least 20 thousand participants including women and children here.

For a time, our youngest son Michael is lost in the crowds but finds his way back to camp. July the 5th 1998 is the day for Pickett's Charge. About 7,000 Confederates will charge about 5,000 Federals. Forty thousand spectators will look on the scene.

Bill Saunders of the 28th writes on a playing card tucked in his hatband, "If I am kilt my family livz in Bedford Viginy. Wm Saunders." Jeff Bower speaks how he read before the charge some men had a feeling they were going to die. Travis White has capsules filled with simulated blood; he will be using the clotting blood today. First Sgt. Jerry Aldhizer carries an authentic 1851 double-barreled coach gun manufactured in France and smuggled through the blockade at Savannah. Mark Musick carries a quilt that belonged to his great-great-great grandfather for a bedroll. General George Pickett's triple great-nephew Ray Pickett leads the charge today. Colonel Dave Cornett uses a cell phone to determine where the Minnesotans are in the Federal line. When we are nearing the wall, we

cut across in front of many of our troops in order to hit the Yanks where the 1st Minnesota is. Our flag changes hands about six times as flag bearers are 'shot.' Only one soldier's rifle is not picked up. Ed Lee, real name is Robert E. Lee, carries the flag over the wall. I am right beside him. His ancestor carried the flag when it was captured 135 years before. Above is Peggy Aldhizer, Melody and Joan Leviner and Barbara Wood. Below is Bill Brown and Jim Wood.

 I pull off a button from my shell jacket to trade with a Minnesotan. A photo is taken of the two companies and can be found on page three of 'Gettysburg 135th Photographic Review' published by 'The Civil War News'.

I have a gate pass for a Clinton, South Carolina event on October 23-25, 1998. Its 'Stoneman's Raid' and is put on by the Hampton Legion. These folks are highly respected, so what follows, do not take it personally. This is the event, I think, that the 28th Va. voted to attend because it is to be a hard-core campaign affair, no tents. It gets pretty cool at night. Our remedy is to lay logs to burn thus extending our fire pit and making room for us and our blankets to bed down around it. There are no spectators, and no Sutlers; however, two Sutlers break the rules and set up. I guess to their credit, at least, they are far off, so we have to walk a bit to get there. I purchase a fine shirt I'll slowly wear out in the coming years.

Live chickens are let lose to run around. The idea is for the Companies to kill, cook, and eat them. Well, we have some fellows who sneak off in their vehicles and bring back lots of fried chicken from some restaurant. Well, needless to say the only way we like to eat it was while walking by the other companies as they look impressed.

We fought skirmish type battles until it gets dark. Well, the next morning we get down to business. Our enemy lives on a hillside and they are still in their camp. The base of the hill is covered in briers, except for the narrow dirt road entrance. Our company concentrates there, and we rush up into the mountain into the midst of their fine-looking camp. It is no telling how long it took them to dig those holes, to make those shelters, but it's over quick. I'm sure some events I have forgotten but this is not one of them even though I don't have pictures.

I go to a Grant vs. Lee Event at Brandy Station, a 135th Anniversary Reenactment. I have a pass but don't remember it. This is June 18-20, 1999. August 27-29, 1999, is the Battle of Saltville, Va. hosted by the 64th Va. Cavalry. This is a small event I attend a few times over the years. There is an old school replica that maybe represents where J.E.B. Stuart's wife taught. Some of the Stuarts are buried at the town. The reenactment is held at the bottom of a natural 'bowl' as mountains surround. Some people still boil the water in pots and get salt.

On this January 8, 2000, five members of the Wharton-Stuart Sons of Confederate Veterans Camp #1832 are in attendance of the flag rally at the South Carolina State Capitol building at Columbia. Jay Shelor, my brothers Eddie and Judson, my sons John and Michael, and I are here for this tremendous event. After arriving, I learn this is a weekend event. On Friday and Saturday, over 20,000 names are read out of South Carolina soldiers who died in the war, one of which is an ancestor of mine. After a brief ceremony, the march starts from Elmwood Cemetery about one and a quarter miles away from the Capitol. Just before we step off, a man informs us that they have just been informed that the parade permit cost $7,500.00. He tells us to enjoy every step. Clergymen with a banner that reads 'No King but Jesus' leads the way. The last Confederate widow is pushed in her wheelchair. It has already been worth the trip to see her. While marching on Main Street, I just have to steal a few glances at our reflections in the plate glass windows. I neither encounter or hear of any hecklers on our entire march. The closer we get to the Capitol the more our supporters and their cheers grow. Shortly after our arrival, a black man in a Confederate uniform with a large Confederate flag on his shoulder comes down in front of our ranks, it is a delightful scene. He is H.K. Edgerton and soldiers are stepping out to hug him. He then faces the crowd with his arms spread wide and says, 'my compatriots, my compatriots' as he looks at us. Then the crowds press in, I hear later 6,000 people. Jerry and Peggy Aldhizer are here also. Jerry stood beside me; believe me he is a camera magnet. Before the speeches get going good, Jerry and Jud take a few moments to go up on the Capitol steps to view the crowd with their wives. This scene is enough to make my S.C.V. Color Sergeant's heart leap for joy. The capitol steps are draped with one huge Confederate flag plus hundreds of others being handheld flags. A man in the ranks behind me even thinks he is in Heaven. During the speeches, our hats barely stayed on our heads as we wave them aloft and cheer often. I think our three crisp volleys add a nice touch, and I can still hear the echo of the crowd saying, 'never take it down' as in my mind's eye I can still see the Confederate flag flying atop the Capitol dome. Since that day, people filled with hate have it removed. But I hear as a result, all of South Carolina's Confederate statures are now protected by law.

Next photo by Paul Collins

In January of 2000, I attend the Lee Jackson Day commemoration held in Lexington, Virginia, to which I have attended numerous times. I walk in the parade from the cemetery that 'Stonewall' Jackson is buried to down near Lee chapel where General Lee is buried. At its front door is where the photo of Jud and I is taken by 28th member Paul Collins. The 28th Va. Infantry is here this year. As a company we march over in front of V.M.I. for a photo. We have Jackson's statue centered behind us in front of the Institution he taught at before going off to war. This is the last time some of us are with the company for soon the 51st is started.

September of 2000 is the battle of Chancellorsville, held at Ft. Pickett, Virginia. About this time, a sort of liability and or accident coverage went in place for members of Longstreet's Corps. Arthur 'Art' C. Wingo is the initial director. Art is one of the ole timers that gets my respect.

Confederate Memorial Day is celebrated in Stuart in 2000.

November of 2001 and I am way down in South Carolina. This event always falls the next weekend after Ft. Branch, well almost every year. Once I ride all the way down to Charleston to find I was a weekend early. They would not let me sleep the night on the grounds of the Boone Hall Plantation, in back of my pickup so I go to a camp ground.

This Battle of Secessonville event I attend quite a few times, as do Jud and my boys.   I have fond memories of the 28th Va. Infantry at this event.

Once I lose my car keys here and only find them after a lock smith had me more made. It is here I purchase a first edition book from a fellow on black slave owners in the state of South Carolina; he says the man in the state who owned the most was a free black man from France. There are nine preserved brick slave quarters on this property. It has a cotton dock used for dances. Under the huge live oak trees that line the plantation entrance are, without a doubt, one of the biggest crowds of Sutlers of any event I have been to, good ones, too.   More often than not, when I am in this area, I go to see Ft. Moultrie and look out at Ft. Sumpter in the harbor, before returning to home in Stuart, Virginia.

Sometimes the poncho was used even by the kids.

One year, Dakota Lytle comes down with his parents Jimmy and Anna, along with Lynell, Michael, and myself. We go see the CSS H. L. Hunley.

The early 2000's are hard times on the home front and my midlife crisis hits hard. After adjusting to a new company, it won't be long before I'll have a couple more difficult experiences in my life. My wife of nineteen years walks out on me. I also go through job transitions, from sawmill work to telephone work, to truck driving work.

On April 17, 2004, Jud and I make it our business to attend the burial of the last crew of the Confederate submarine H. L. Hunley, in Charleston, South Carolina's Magnolia cemetery. We park then catch a bus to the Battery. We step off the bus and are relieved to see a familiar face in Terry Shelton. The procession starts at White Point Gardens and goes four point five miles to Magnolia cemetery. Jud and I wear wool Confederate uniforms and it is a hot low country day. We both don't feel too good physically. On the 8th day of this month, I had wrecked the 18-wheeler I was driving for Gregory Pallet & Lumber Company, in a sharp curve in Stokes Co. N.C., laying over the truck and flatbed with 616 pallets. I had not driven a year yet. The resulting 14 stitches in the top of my head has left me now still in a weaken state, I think.

An estimated crowd of between 75 to 300 thousand people are on hand, according to security personal. No arrests are made by the way. We all are honored and sadden to be here. These eight men are laid to rest after being released from the submarine their bodies had stayed in for so many decades.

This event of a lifetime is made largely possible and done with this much dignity due to two men in my opinion, Randy Burbage of South Carolina, and Henry Kidd of Virginia. I am blessed to have reenacted with both men before. I wish you all could read the March/April issue of the Confederate Veteran magazine which details this event, and from which I get some details. I leave with you the names of the eight men who succeeded in sinking the U.S.S. Housatonic: Lt. George E. Dixon, Seaman Arnold Becker, Crewman C. Simpkin, Seaman Frank G. Collins, Corporal J. F. Carlsen, Seaman Miller, Boatswain Mate James A. Wicks, and Quartermaster Joseph F. Ridgeway.

Long-time friend and ole college buddy, Don Lewellyn, and I embark on telephone work together. He knows this type of work inside and out. We also start a company of the 24th Va. Infantry. We shine at places such as New Market, Saltville, and J.E.B. Stuart's Birthplace. Of the ten companies of the 24th Va., one was from Patrick County, Va. where I live. We are told someone else has all the rights to the 24th so, for a while, we are representing the 45th N.C. Infantry. We are at the 140th Gettysburg Anniversary event in 2003.

All these years, the companies would have their Camps of the Instructions. These are held before the 'reenacting season' begins meaning a cold time of the year. Perhaps it is the cold that I seem to remember the most. The 28th Virginia Infantry Co. C Craig Mountain boys of which I am a member of roughly seven

years, held the hardiest of all my time in reenacting. Up in the mountains in much isolation and extreme cold for the most part and marching on mountain sides, we train. The road to get there is a dirt road that crosses a creek numerous times. Once or twice I wondered if my 1995 Lumina is going to float away. On one occasion, Jud and I leave early as more rain is coming. We dig 'sinks' and a cabin is even built by some of the soldiers. I never get to sleep in it but hear it is warm inside. It is pretty full, even the loft, of people escaping the cold. The early Camps of the Instruction for the 51st Va. are held here. A rat takes up residence in the cabin and gets the nickname 'Confeder rat'. Out near one of the Otter rivers on another Camp of the Instruction, I have to practically stand in the fire at night to combat the bitter cold. A Camp of the Instruction held by the 51st one time is up near the top of the mountain on Belcher's Mt. Road at the site of a place of a famous 'Civil War' author, Burke Davis.

On June 26, 2004 Lynell and I are married. After our marriage, I return to the ranks of the 51st Va.; she becomes involved looking much the part in a hoop skirt. Her first event as a participant is at New Market, Va., in May of 2005. Sammy Hughes's wife and children are very helpful and kind, welcoming her in. We sleep the first night on the usual gum blanket with a blanket or quilt. The second night, lots of hay is added. I am having to change some of my old ways. She is impressed by the number of our troops and we will go on to enjoy years of reenacting together as it is my wish for her to see what it is like.

On April, 29, 2006 Confederate Memorial Day is observed in Patrick County Va. at the old Courthouse in Stuart. Our Wharton-Stuart Sons of Confederate Veterans camp #1832 have two speakers that turns into three for this event.

Thomas D. Perry who holds a B.A. in Virginia Tech speaks on Patrick Confederate soldiers. Tom is the Free State of Patrick: Patrick County In 1990, Mr. Perry started the J. E. Birthplace Preservation Trust, Inc. from Asheville, N.C. speaks on his preserve Confederate history. The wearing a Confederate uniform has also. history from Counties author of The in The Civil War. B. Stuart H. K. Edgerton efforts to black man our attention

 His brother is our unexpected next speaker. We move over to Dehart Park next for a 'pig picking' with live music.

Many are the good times and many are the memories that never get told. For some reason not known to me, I start keeping a journal in 2007 and, like Lynell, I would like to include you in knowing what it is like.

CHAPTER 2 - 2007

Early on this January the 13th day in 2007, Lynell and I go to Lexington, Virginia, commemorating Lee- Jackson Day. This January marks General Lee's 200th birthday and Stonewall's 183rd birthday. We assemble with the crowd up at 'Stonewall' Jackson's grave. Colors are presented by the Maryland Division Sons of Confederate Veterans Color Guard. Next come songs, prayers' a speaker then a volley is fired. Afterward, we walk in a procession from there to V.M.I. campus parade ground for another speech. We are in period clothes for this event, and I get great pictures. From here, Lynell and I make it over to the museum in the basement of the V.M.I. chapel. We walk to the Lee chapel on the grounds of Washington and Lee University.

Last year, we sat inside through the wonderful speeches, but this year we sit outside and hear from loudspeakers. We walk back up into town and have lunch. After lunch, we walk back to the car, drive to the Visitor Center, and change clothes. We walk to 'Stonewall' Jackson's house where Lynell takes a tour, I had taken one year before. General Lee's birthday arrives on the 19 of January.

On February the 3rd of 2007, we attend the annual meeting of the 51st Va. Inf. being held this year at the Patrick Springs, Virginia Volunteer Fire Department. We bring food that Lynell spent parts of yesterday and today preparing. The year's events we vote for after our Camp of Instruction in March are Bedford, then known as Liberty, New Market, Gettysburg, Zackery Hill, and J.E.B. Stuart's birthplace. On February the 26th of 2007 for $500.15, we get our own tent which is a white canvas 6x9x8 A frame tent.

On March the 3rd of 2007, I leave my house to arrive at the J.E.B. Stuart birthplace about 45 minutes later. I sit out under the full moon awhile. First

Sergeant Williams drives up. We walk over to the camp and will eventually make a fire. The camp begins stirring and I am given the task of having the morning Colors posted. We go through the Manuel of Arms, Stacking Arms, drilling, and marching. I think everyone gets a crack at commanding the company. When Allen Jackson finishes, I am in tears from laughing. Captain Harris is hiding his face in his hands. A group of the ladies brings us soup we heat atop of the fire grate. Sammy Hughes's kids and other kids also are at play. We have a tactical fight on a steep hillside. Even before it is over, and especially afterwards, everyone is talking how many times they shot so and so.

S.C.V. Virginia State Convention is held in Martinsville this year.

Today is April the 14th of 2007. I have been a member of the Sons of Confederate Veterans since November 28, 1992, which doesn't require its members to have uniforms but I choose to have one which helps at grave marker dedications and posting of colors, for example. Our ancestors did not fight or die in vain. We honor the memory of their sacrifice, their struggle for independence, their love of the South and all her people. Lynell, wearing a hoop skirt, comes with me as I wear my Confederate uniform. At the old Henry County Courthouse, I join in the Color Guard. My brother Judson is here. Wharton-Stuart members are here to help out the Stuart-Hairston camp.

The main convention although is mostly in the Dutch Inn in Collinsville, Virginia. We listen to speeches and, before we leave, fire three of the best volleys I have ever heard.

April is Confederate History Month, and the next Saturday finds me at the old Patrick County Court House in Stuart, Virginia. Lynell and I are there early. I join four others in a ceremony of lowering the 'American' flag and the Patrick County flag from half mast, then raising the 2ⁿᵈ National Confederate flag to half-mast. Later, we return to observe Confederate Memorial Day, beginning at 11 A.M. Our Commander Chris Washburn and President of the J.E.B. Stuart Preservation Trust speak. Judson and I are in the Honor Guard that fire three volleys. A wreath is placed in front of the stature of a Confederate soldier. We have a pig picking in the nearby park!

April proves to be a busy month. We are at Bedford, Va. on the 27ᵗʰ day of this 2007. We set up our tent and it is good to get in uniform again. Lynell's brother Harold Jones comes over and visits from Forest, Va.; with him are his wife Margie, his son Doug, his daughter-in-law Dee, his daughter Shawn, and his granddaughter, Kaylee. I talk to Dave Lawhorn and Sonny Bishop of the 28ᵗʰ Va. Infantry Co. C Craig Mountain Boys. This night is the first we spend in our new tent. There are some high winds. The metal pegs, in the tops of the uprights, are its strength.

This morning, we have Roll Call, Post Colors, have breakfast, drill, have a Dress Parade, then more drill. Back in camp, we show pictures and take pictures.

Sammy and Michelle's children are here.

Lynell and I have lunch in the tent. At 12:30, there is an Ammo Call. I get three bags of rounds and one container of caps. Then comes First Call and

forming for battle. In so doing, we are filmed by battle documentary cameras. The battle starts in front of the Elks Home. A few cannons are involved. The Yankees are supposed to win today even though there are fewer of them. I never do take a 'hit.' At the end of the battle, the nipple on my rifle becomes so clogged that it is not firing. I replace it with a spare when I clean it.

Our first and former 51st Va. Captain Jerry Aldhizer and his wife Peggy stop by for a visit. Lynell and I have supper in the tent then distribute some 8x10's to the 24th guys.

Its April 29, 2007, and I sleep well, when I sleep. There is trouble with the air mattress leaking. We have the usual morning Roll Call. I get in another shave. This is my 75th reenactment and the first time I ever recall shaving at one. The Colors are posted. We had drill and then a Dress Parade at 10 o'clock. In our camp we have church, Allen Jackson delivers the sermon. Sammy Hughes has some leftover ham and potatoes that Lynell and I help him out with. Eventually, we go out to wait for battle. We get into the business part of town, pushing the Yankees. At one point we go after some in an alleyway, shoot, then turn around to 'shoot' more. Both sets of Federals are being 'pushed' by our troops. The Yankees are eventually hemmed in and captured. Spectators watch the thing unfold. We load up and leave out.

On the 18th of May, it is my turn to give brother Jud a ride to an event. We meet up to go to New Market, Virginia. Tomorrow, schoolteacher Lynell must be at the High School Graduation where she teaches so she is unable to go with us. When we arrive, it is drizzling rain so we stay under the camper shell. The next morning, Jud and I pack up the truck and go to find our camp. I carry a gum blanket and gray blanket bedroll on me and tote the extra rifle and bayonet I have for Allen Jackson to use. We are at Roll Call and I am on the Color detail. Eventually, there is a Dress Parade. Three of us Stack Arms and go to the Sutlers. Last night, I got a spare nipple for my rifle. I get a refrigerator magnet for Lynell of Confederate flags. I go back to the truck eat and start drying out in the sun the tent and poncho used last night on back of the truck to make our space bigger. I go over to the Museum and run into Jud. Back at camp, we are told to accouter up and are rushed out to skirmish the Yankees beyond the Bushong house. We have a pretty good time roughing them up. They go back to camp. We go back to camp, then right back out again. This time we are in with the main Confederate force. In the fighting, I take an early 'hit,' having expanded a lot of ammo already. We have a fellow originally from England fight with us.

Today is Sunday the 27th of May 2007, a day Veterans are honored at our church, the Buffalo Ridge Pentecostal Holiness Church. In 1983 at age 24, I was Honorably discharged from active duty in the United States Marine Corps. Because I have worked hard and lost 53 pounds, I am able to get into my old Dress Blues.

In church, I carry a Christian flag as part of a Memorial Service. Later in the day, I put on the uniform of a Confederate soldier and drive to Danbury, North Carolina. On the grounds of the old historic Courthouse, the 17th annual Tribute to Stokes County Confederate Veterans is carried out. I am one of thirteen rifles on the Honor Guard commanded by a sword toting captain.

We Stack Arms twice and fire
three volleys. Speeches are delivered
and refreshments served. Tomorrow is
Memorial Day; it began as Decoration
Day to remember 'Civil War' soldiers.

On July the 6th 2007, wife Lynell and
I travel to Pennsylvania for the
144th Anniversary of the battle of
Gettysburg. We drive into the town of Gettysburg via Fairfield route. We tour some of the original battlefield. We see the Virginia monument and the new equestrian statue of General James Longstreet.

Despite the crowds, we find the reenactment site, but get caught up in the thousands of spectators coming in for a battle that is about to start. We finally set up while they are out to battle. Earlier, a tent and its contents burn up as it is too close to a fire pit. It is in the next company over from us. Lynell buys a classy black hat and black belt when we go to the Sutlers.

July the 7th, 2007, also my oldest brother Eddie's birthday, finds us up early

for breakfast. I'm happy we did because things get going and some don't have a chance to eat. We have Roll Call, a Weapons Inspection, and form for battle. We are the first ones on the field as usual. This is a tactical battle. We march about two miles, I guess, into an area I remember being in four years ago. Our battalion stages in the woods. I am one of three scouts sent out. The main Federal army does not come in the area we scouted, but their cavalry is out doing some scouting of their own. Later on, I learn one of us was captured. The last thing I remember telling the boy was do not let the Cavalry see you! After the battle, I rejoin our men and we 'drive' the Yankees awhile. We march back to camp through the Sutlers. We clean rifles and eat. After resting a bit, Lynell and I walk to the Sutlers. We get a spoon and a nail keg. This barrel looking keg will be used to house the 3-pound hammer and metal tent stakes.

After we get back, I form up for inspection. The 51st Va. marches out to a Dress Parade. We are part of Longstreet Corps and our company sponsored by the 1st Kentucky. Next, we march out in front of the thousands of spectators in the stands for the five o'clock battle. Our company has two guys from New Jersey falling in with us this weekend.

One is using my spare rifle. I don't die in this battle. Back in camp, Lynell fixes chicken and dumplings.

This morning, we make the early Porta-John trips then have breakfast in our tent. We both had a good night's sleep and I shave when it is light enough to do so. There is Roll Call and our Colors are posted. Boys of the 63rd Tenn. are being sponsored by us and are posting their Colors with ours. Some of our soldiers post the Headquarters' flag. We move out on a dirt road to stand in the shade for the morning Dress Parade. Here a most likeable sergeant of the 1st Kentucky, I know as Sam, receives the Longstreet Corps Soldier of the Year award. Often have I heard his laughter about camp and can identify him by it. General Moffin says that he would be on furlough for the rest of the year. His health is not good. General Dan Shumate takes charge and leads us later in Pickett's charge. Back in camp we talk and have Church Service before lunch. Pvt. Allen Jackson preaches, and Pvt. Milton leads in prayer and song. We assemble and get in place for a two o'clock reenacting of Pickett's Charge. There is a heat casualty before it can start. Ice that is handed out goes down the backs of shirts and under hats. This turns out to be a disappointing charge. I honestly don't think I see one Yankee go down, and the ground is littered with Confederates. We didn't get to the wall.

It is the 21st of July 2007, and it is time for this year's 51st Virginia's Camp for Kids held here at the Reynolds Homestead in Critz, Virginia, in Patrick County. I leave from home and soon arrive to see a Confederate flag flying at the head of a company street of tents. First Sgt. Terry Williams comes marching with 14 boys behind him, and Allen Jackson behind them. Captain Harris and 1st Lt. Harrell are here. Later, Pete and son Doug Camper come in from Roanoke with a friend. The boys are here for a two-day camp to learn about the life of Confederate soldiers and, hopefully, more of the War Between the States. A reporter from 'The Roanoke Times' comes out, and we all get photographed. I show and tell about my maimed hand since it involved a muzzle loader. The kids learn drill and how to march. We go in the Learning Center and see a film on 'Stonewall' Jackson and 1st Manassas. I leave to return tomorrow.

When I arrive back here the next morning, I see Allen Jackson. He informs me the captain left early for home being sick. We carry on the rest of the time without him. Terry Williams then Lester Harrell come in. Later Mrs. Anita, Lester's wife, and Bremen, their son, come in. This is Bremen's 16th birthday. They bring jackets and hats. I believe we have a jacket, hat, coat, or vest for each of the 13 boys. One has left. We get old stakes, like tomato stakes, for the boys to use as guns. It's more drill and practicing. The boys practice giving commands, some at various ranks. Allen Jackson conducts a morning Church service. At ten A.M., we fall in and march. A Dress Parade is conducted for the parents who have arrived and are seated in chairs on the lawn. The young soldiers now return the articles of Confederate uniforms. I give one young man the first hat I ever had in reenacting. It is a gray bummer style kepi, I obtained from Pete Camper.

The Zackery Hill event is held at Snow Camp, North Carolina. I arrive on the evening of the 21st Of September 2007. Lynell is at home this weekend in order to teach Sunday School. I have help setting up the tent. I help dig a fire pit and carry firewood. A Sutler gives me this candle that I am writing by.

The next morning, I awake here having slept all alone in our big tent. We have a formation, Colors are posted. At 8:30 A.M. we form again, this time for company drill and from there, we go into Battalion formation for Dress Parade. After this, more company drill. The day is sweltering hot. At 11 A.M., Terry Shelton is married to his bride in the camp of the 1st Kentucky about 30 yards from my tent! Susan takes some pictures for me. I can't keep up with Mr. Shelton's rank but he is the overall Confederate commander here. I have some soup for lunch after which we have an Ammo Call. We get First Call 51st Virginia, get accoutrements on, then fall in with our rifles to get inspected. We march to the staging area. My friend H.K. Edgerton is here, and we shake hands. This black man in a Confederate uniform leads us in to battle the Yankees, as he waves his Confederate battle flag. We whipped the Yankees soundly. Back in camp, the 51st sets about cleaning rifles. Over to the next street in the camp of the 1st Ky., we go. Some honors are given out called 'Kentucky Colonels.' I go to Sutler Row and take pictures of H.K. with his flag and a black lady in period attire.

Later, reenactors are served a free meal.

Early on this 23rd day of September 2007, I am on my way to the Porta-John when I hear the first bird of the day. I get my canteen filled from the spigot on the water line running along the fence. Soon, a fire is built, and Company Colors are posted. Some of us meander off to get breakfast. I talk to Doug Camper awhile, he is our officer today, a Lieutenant. Our captain left last evening. We form up and march out for Dress Parade. It is another sunny and even hotter day than yesterday. The galvanized Yankees join us as before. Not long after, we have Church Call at the big tent. Nathan Black's dad spoke on 'the myth of adolescence, the significance of ages 12 and 30' with Jesus as our example. The preacher was raised in Hawaii. He studied in Jerusalem, Israel. He has been a missionary to Ethiopia. In two weeks, he plans to travel to Iran to speak to Muslims. We grab a little lunch. We form up to go out and stage for the 2 o'clock battle. H.K. leads the Confederates into battle waving his Confederate battle flag.

It is Thursday the 4th of October 2007 when I arrive at the J.E.B. Stuart birthplace in Ararat, Virginia, here in Patrick County. Mike Pendleton helps set up my tent. I help set up our Wharton- Stuart Sons of Confederate Veterans tent.

The next evening after our 'day jobs' are finished; Lynell and I are soon on our way to Ararat. We let Registration use our candle powered lantern. We put our stuff in the tent. Doug Camper comes in; I help him set up. I get to speak to Officer Greg Gallion who comes in. We are camped below the Pavilion where I have not camped before. We hear cars from a dirt track in the distance.

This is Saturday the 6th of October, 2007, where we awake, on Laurel Hill. I can remember coming to early events here held in June. We fall in for Roll Call and Company Colors are posted also. I find my brother Judson came in earlier and slept using a ground cloth and blanket. This is the 17th year of this event and he has been in attendance at every one. I remember stopping out on the roadside when he was too young to drive so he could get out to explore in this area. It was so overgrown along the road then that I could not see over in here.

We form for Dress Parade and afterward have Battalion Drill. Here is high ranking Officers Dave Cornett and Greg Gallion.

Back in my 28th Va. Inf. Days, they were my Captain and Lieutenant. Other members of those days in the 28th are here visiting. These include Jerry Aldhizer, Jim Wood, Jeff Bower, and Don Whitaker. Jerry, Jim, and Don's wives and Jeff's son Erik are here as well. Peggy Aldhizer and Barbara Wood were part of the Ma Wood gang that tried to keep our 'chicken thief' Terry Williams in line. Other memories of the 28th at this place include the night battles. Ed Lee use to help out by bringing night vision hardware. A flare high in the night sky would expose our enemy sneaking across an open field, so they ran like cock roaches. Erik would turn out to make a good soldier and bagpipe player.

Lynell and I eat some Indian frybread over at the Sutlers where I also buy a jean cloth kepi. We get confined to camp. Soon, it's Ammo Call, then First Call, then form for battle. We stage in the woods. The Ararat Rescue Squad picks up a casualty before a shot is fired. We start out in the field but go back into the woods where I get scratched up with briars. We are reenacting a round top scenario today and the Yanks win. The 51st Va. has around 22 rifles in our company today. We eat barbeque. Colors are retired. We host the candlelight tour. I am wounded sometimes and a dead soldier sometimes as various groups come through to witness the horrors of war.

October the 7th, 2007, dawns cold. Early on I get the ole canteen filled with water. At Roll Call, Bremen and Patrick answer from inside their tents. Colors are posted and we eat breakfast. At 10:30 A.M., the 51st Va. Has Church Call at the Captain's tent fly. Corporal, as of this weekend, Allen Jackson preaches and leads the Communion Service. Helping out are Doug and Milton. Travis White closes in prayer. Lynell and I listen as Mike Pendleton plays a guitar and sings.

We have a Company Meeting. Officers are voted on for the first time here at 'J.E.B. Stuart.' They all remain the same. Lieutenant Harrell suggests we have annual elections here. Later, we form for battle under Captain Harris, with 1st Sgt. Williams directing us on the field. We fire and charge through our own camp, driving the Yankees into the open on the other side of the Sutlers. The 51st is divided into two big squads in our fighting place in the Confederate Army.

Lieutenant Harrell's squad is involved in 'Guard Against Cavalry'. I see when he is stepped on by a horse. Judson is captured. We come along to free him and capture two cannons. The battle ends and 'taps' play as we Uncover. My head is bowed, my hat in hand, when my eyes spot a spider stirred up by the battle. I talk with Captain Russell about running. He is very fit for a man of his age.

On the 15th of October 2007, Lynell and I visit Sean and Tanya Verlik's house, where once I attended a 51st Va. Infantry Company Meeting. Lynell purchases five dress outfits, two shawls, two purses, and three pairs of period drawers.

This second day of November 2007 finds the two of us traveling to West Virginia. We arrive at this place called Huntington beside of the Ohio River; we're here for the Guyandotte event. I talked to some 36th Va. fellows to camp and fall in with. We get set up across from the V.F.W. building. I get a vest for $25.00 and give $24.00 to Lynell to buy me a Derby hat as I have said I will not buy any more hats; they are my weakness. I sew on two buttons and put powder in tubes. Corporal Brown and later Terry and Joan Williams come in. We enjoy pizza from the corner Pizzeria. We sit around the campfire and talk. I mess up a good writing pen using it to work on our lantern.

We get out of our tents this morning to frost on the ground. After warming by the fire, Lynell and I go in at the V.F.W. building to join others for breakfast. Two members, other than I, of the 'Wharton-Stuart' Sons of Confederate Veterans camp #1832 and their wives are here. The biscuit, gravy, hot chocolate, and hot coffee are good. Shortly after our return to camp, I fall in with the 36th Virginia for drill on the Manual of Arms, then Skirmish Drill. There is no posting of Colors or Dress Parade. A little later, we fall back in for a Manual of Arms demonstration/lecture for a group of one to two hundred school kids. The young people are educated about the life of the soldier.

We go to the First Guyandotte Baptist Church for a free lunch of soup, cornbread, and all the fixings. This time, I fall in for drill with the 5th Virginia; Doug Camper is now here and in charge of this company. Lynell and Joan Williams get books at a library book fair. Before long, we form for battle; this is fought in the streets, lots, and back yards in this area of town. A 13-year-old, brace-wearing lad, who lied about his age, fires a loud 50 caliber rifle by my side. We capture a bunch of Yankees. We clean rifles as Indian drums are being beat on down the street. Lynell and I take a walk. At five P.M., there is more drill. At 6 P.M., we attend a Candle/Lamp Light Service. At 8 P.M., the Military Banquet is held at the V.F.W. building.

November 4, 2007, another cold night is past. We are comfortable in the tent. A loud-mouthed drunk coming by only woke us up once. We take breakfast this morning in the Methodist Church basement down the street. Sons of

Confederate Veteran member Larry Cassidy and his wife take it with us. After a while, we go to the First Baptist Church for Sunday School. At 11 A.M., a Memorial Service for Veterans is held, the local R.O.T.C. participate. We Stack Arms and hang around camp. The Yankees come attacking through camp. We fire and fall back a lot. Lynell is with the women yelling at the Yankees. After the battle, we break camp, having to carry our stuff out because the street remains closed. It takes us several trips. We cross over into Ohio before heading home.

This is now the tenth day of November 2007 and also the 3rd annual Patrick County Veterans Parade. Parades usually begin between Hutchens Petroleum and the Wood Brothers Racing Museum, however, this one starts in the SunTrust Bank parking lot.

We turn by the old Courthouse wearing our Confederate uniforms proudly as we Present Arms and Eyes Right to the Confederate statue that represents Confederate veterans. Also, in the parade honoring Veterans are the V.F.W. Veterans, the Patrick County High School J.R.O.T.C., the Boy Scouts, and one man representing a Revolutionary War soldier. The parade continues on down Main Street, a turn by the jewelry store, up Slusher, and to the Veteran's building lot.

On December 2, 2007, the annual Stuart, Virginia Christmas Parade is held. Lynell drops me off at the Stuart Primitive Baptist Church parking lot where the Wharton- Stuart S.C.V. camp #1832 stage for the parade. I remember first marching in the parade in the late 90's. Before that, I was a spectator watching the 2nd Va. Cav. on horseback with usually a J.E.B. Stuart reenactor leading them. Now, this will be the first time I remember riding on a trailer 'float.' In my uniform, I throw candy with the others. Twice we fired double loads into the air.

Still in December of 2007, this is the 15th and our S.C.V. Christmas Banquet. In the evening, Lynell and I dress for the activities ahead. She wears a riding dress and hoop skirt outfit. I employ grey frock coat and trousers, thin black cotton tie tied in a bow, and a black derby hat. We go to the Stuart Rotary field house where the Patrick County Music Association is having its monthly gathering. Our S.C.V. Commander is catering barbeque, slaw, beans, and the trimmings for a camp fund raiser. Lynell and I are door greeters. Later on, we go over to the Reynold's Homestead on this icy, rainy night for the banquet.

CHAPTER 3 - 2008

Lynell and I travel to Lexington, Virginia, to the Lee-Jackson Day Commemoration. We dress in period attire as do many others here. In the hilltop graveyard where 'Stonewall' Jackson is buried, the wreath laying ceremony is just underway.

Afterward, we march in a parade through town that ends on the V.M.I. Parade Deck.

Several Sons of Confederate Veteran camps are represented in the parade. Lynell and I go in the museum to view the rain slicker Jackson was wearing the night he was shot.

We sit in the upstairs chapel before going over to the Lee Chapel. As a service is going on, we go to the basement and view crypts of some of Lee's family members and enter the museum too before we leave.

The annual meeting of the 51st Va. Co. D is today the second of February, 2008, and is being held in the Patrick Springs, Virginia Volunteer Fire Department building. We carry in loads of food Lynell has cooked plus a photo album of most of last year's events. The 1996 video of Gettysburg at Fairfield gets some viewing. We learn that my ole Captain Dave Cornett is now our new Longstreet Corps Commander. He is the best man for the job and has my support. The Company votes to go to: Bedford, April 25-27; New Market, May 16-18; Gettysburg 145th, July 4-6; J.E.B. Stuart, October 3-5; Cedar Creek, October 17-19; and Lynell and I are thinking about going to Chickamauga 145th, September 19-21.

The first day 0f March, 2008, our Camp of Instruction is held at the Major General J.E.B. Stuart birthplace in Ararat, Virginia. I arrive on site the evening before, and Cpl. Brown helps me set up the tent. Before the night is over, I am wearing five layers of upper body clothing, a thick pair of trousers, two pair of socks and brogans. I also am using two ground clothes, two blankets, two quilts, two pillows, and a comforter. The ground is frosty as the wind finally laid some. Some members of the 51st Va. Infantry Company D come in this morning. We have Roll Call, Colors posted, and a fire built. With our accouterments on, we go out to drill. Practicing by Files Left, By Files Right, By the Right Flank, By the Left Flank, March by Company into Line, At the Right and At the Left Oblique March, Stack Arms, and other maneuvers. We come back to camp, Stack Arms and police the area. Some go to the camp of the 1st Kentucky, who are here also for breakfast. We take the field for more drill: Shoulder Arms, Right Shoulder Shift, Order Arms, always from the Left Shoulder position, as Present Arms, and Arms Port. We Left Wheel and Right Wheel and Counter March by files Left and Right. Each man takes a turn at marching the company. This is one of Captain Bobby Harris's directives. Those taking the turn at being in charge are Lt. Harrell, 1st Sgt. Williams, Cpl. Brown, and Privates Underwood, Harrell, Wells, Pendleton, and myself.

In the nearby camp of the 1st Kentucky, there is at least fifteen people. We scout them out. 1st Sgt Williams sneaks into the camp and puts on a woman's cape. We fire into their camp, but they do not fire back. Several of us leave this evening.

This is the 29th of March, 2008, and I get involved in cemetery clean-up work. At Dry Pond, Virginia, I meet up with about a dozen members of our Wharton-Stuart S.C.V. camp #1832.

In eight vehicles, we travel toward Collinstown, Virginia. This is where, in 1976 as a 17-year-old, I worked hard at a portable sawmill set there to saw out a band of timber. Today, we turn off to the right in sight of the North Carolina State line. It takes a while for us to even get to the graveyard to start working due to the terrain, the size of vehicles, smallness of fence gates, etc. Larry Cassidy has his brother joining us today. We get up to a wooded cemetery filled with brush and broken headstones. Amid off and on drizzle on this cold cloudy day, we clean, cut, drag and toss brush, briars, etc. Three, sometimes four, strands of barb wire go around, we enclose several rock graves left out of the old fence.

 A little wire entrance gate is made. Each of the three Confederate Veterans buried here get a Confederate flag.

On April 5, 2008, Judson and I represent our S.C.V. camp at the old Martinsville, Va. Courthouse. We join the Stuart-Hairston S.C.V. camp #515 in their Confederate Memorial Day observance. Neither Camp Commanders are present. Three volleys are fired as part of it.

On April 19, 2008, I participate in our Wharton-Stuart S.C.V. camp #1832 Confederate Memorial Day observance at the old Patrick County Courthouse. Four of us stand on the old Courthouse steps. Author Gary Walker is the guest speaker. A wreath is laid at the Confederate statue on the lawn. We fire three perfect volleys. At last, I get to move out of the glare coming from off the windshield of a parked van.

We arrive at Bedford, Virginia, on the 25th of April 2008. After we register, we see Corporals Jackson and Brown who tell us where our camp is. Lewis Steppe and his family are here. After our tent is set up Lt. Harrell and most of his family come in. We all help him set up a wall tent, tent fly, and two A frame tents. It has really been raining.

This is Saturday the 26th of April, and we awake with the early birds chirping. The encampment slowly comes to life. Judson comes in and we have a Roll Call. People start getting breakfast. The soldiers get ready for Company Drill. Next comes a Longstreet Corps Dress Parade. We are addressed by our new Commander General Cornett. Officer Gallion is in charge of this event. I talk to the now Captain of the 28th Va., Sonny Bishop, and Lt. Dave Lawhorn. After Dress Parade, Lynell and I go to the three Sutlers. She gets some dress sleeves, a couple of plates, and candles. I buy an historic novel from its author Henry Kidd. He signs the work entitled <u>Petersburg War on the Doorsteps,</u> an historic novel where all the history is true.

Back at camp, we get an Ammo Call. Captain Harris came in for the battle and has left. This is the first time for 1st Sgt. Underwood to take the field. His promotion was so quick he wears no stripes. We form for battle and march over to the back side of the Elk's Home, where we have a tactical battle with the Yankees. First Texas is first company, and we are second company. These two companies are skirmishing the whole time. Afterwards, we have lunch down by the pond. I am detailed and go with Cpl. Jackson to fill canteens with water from a spigot on an old building. Former 51st Va. Captain Jerry Aldhizer and his grandson come in to join us. With our company at about a dozen now, we march to confront our foe once again. After coming around in back of the Elks Home, we are deployed as skirmishers. As the artillery is going in, I help push one of the big guns awhile. We go on up and start firing. At our farthest point of skirmish, Cpl. Brown, Judson, Lewis Steppe, and I take 'hits.' As I lay here, I hear one causality fart. After we get back to camp, rain hits hard. A former 28th Va. Infantry member, Jim Day, comes by. He is the Police Chief of Bedford.

On the morning of the 27th of April 2008, we awake here on the lawn where we camped at old Randolph Macon Academy and Liberty Academy. We have a Bible study under the tent fly. It rained off and on all night. Folks get breakfast when they can, in between and after Roll Call and Dress Parade. Church Call comes and is held at Lt. Harrell's tent fly about twelve feet from our tent. Corporal Allen Jackson delivers the sermon to a good crowd. It's cloudy, but the rain holds off. Mike Pendleton and his wife come in. He joins us for the upcoming battle. The 1st Kentucky leave for town first. Coming into town later, the 28th Va. go up a street, and the 1st Texas and the 51st Va. go up another. They call four of us up to skirmish. We can see the Yanks near the Courthouse. I hear cannon fire, but as far as I know I open up the street fight with the first shot. We advance awhile, then we are replaced by four more skirmishers. The 28th come in from a side street and we 'drive' the Yankees. Doug Camper 'dies' in front of the Courthouse while rushing them. The 1st Kentucky come on from another street and the Yankees surrender. We get back and break camp. Jud helps himself to a big ole turkey leg at the Spring Frolic.

This is Saturday the 3rd of May 2008 and Lynell and I are all decked out in our period attire as we arrive at the Reynolds Homestead here in Critz, Virginia for our first time attending the annual Spring Frolic. Sammy Hughes and his family have set up a couple of tents and some flags. Other members of our Wharton-Stuart Sons of Confederate Veterans camp #1832 are here. Inside of the Events Center is a display. A part of it shows an original letter written by Samuel A.

Dowless, Confederate ancestor of Judson and mine. Also, there are artifacts and a poem I wrote.

Among the activities that can be seen are women weaving wool on spinning wheels, a horse drawn wagon, kids' games, Elmer Dehart doing his Mountain Man impression, and food venders including Southern Traditions run by our Commander Sammy Hughes and Michelle Hughes. Judson and I drill a young man in the Manual of Arms who is a new 51st Va. recruit.

Lynell and I arrive here at New Market, Virginia, on the evening of the 16th of May 2008.

We are greeted by Captain Harris, his wife Brenda, Sgt. Wilson, and Corporals Brown and Jackson. They are gracious to help us set up the tent.

At 5:30, we are up this morning of the 17th of May. We are in sight of Interstate 81 and the roar of traffic is almost constant. I believe I have achieved two firsts here at my 82nd event. We had our passes already and didn't have to go through registration, and it looks, now, like I will be the company's only private this weekend. Colors are not posted, maybe another first outside of Guyandotte. I think this is because we may not have any flags. Lt. Lester Harrell and family and the company ammo are not here due to vehicle trouble. We fall in with the 1st Ky. for Dress Parade, company drill, and battalion drill. Afterwards, Lynell and I go to the Sutlers. Among the things we buy are a bonnet, ammo, caps, a nipple pick, and food. When forming for battle, we fall in with the 1st Kentucky.

The usual long prebattle wait is done standing, I guess just as well as the ground is wet. We march out and form a line of battle in front of the Hall of valor museum.

Amid the roar of cannons, we set out after the Yanks, blazing away as we go. We cross between the Bushong House and the big barn out behind it, on through the peach orchard and into the Field of Lost Shoes. That's where I take a 'hit'; I tell Sgt. Wilson that I am gut shot. This turns out to be a real ammo saving maneuver. I get up and march out with the company at battles end. I cook up some steaks over a fire Captain Harris and I build. As I walk by the front of the Bushong House, I look through the open doors to view the barn out back. At the Sutlers I buy three yards of black wool, two nipple picks, a wooden button, and a John Wayne can opener just like the ones I used to open C rations in my old U.S.M.C. days.

About 2:30 A.M., I awake but Lynell is already awake. A group of people are standing around a fire talking. I put earplugs in to get more sleep. We cook up a skillet of ham and vegetables for breakfast. Today the 51st is down to four, Cpl. Brown went home last night. Cpt. Harris, Sgt. Wilson, Cpl. Jackson, and I go over to the 1st Ky. Company. We have Dress Parade over by the Museum and some drill following. Back at camp, there is Church Call with Cpl. Jackson officiating. Later, he has to go look for a 'worm' for his rifle, it is used to remove stuck cleaning patches from barrels. He didn't find one but what he did find is his girlfriend and her father walking toward camp. It is not long before we go to the 1st Ky. to form for rifle inspection which Capt. Harris presides over. We march over to the museum area. Yesterday, we had two 'fresh fish,' those that have their first battle, today there are two more. One of them is a black Confederate. After the battle started and before we made it to the back of the Bushong House, he is down, and I pass him. Later in the orchard, I look and he is in front of me. I am in the Field of Lost Shoes and get 'wounded'. I make it back to camp. Lynell has brought the pickup and has it loaded. I change, then we take the tent down. We see Allen Jackson and his girlfriend in Harrisonburg on our way back.

On the 25th Of May,2008, I participate in two Memorial Services. This is also Sunday. I march down the center aisle of our Church carrying a Christian flag beside of Richard Pilson, a Vietnam Veteran and also a former boss man. All Vietnam Veterans are my heroes. Megan Hanchey goes before carrying the Bible.

In the afternoon I head South. At Five Forks, I look for Jonathan Wilson's house before going on down into North Carolina. At Danbury, I talk to some people to find out their Memorial Service is to be at 3 P.M. I thought at two, so knowing I can't be two places at once I back track a few miles. So up route 8 across from C.C. Moore's Store off Campbell post office road, I wait for others to arrive. I am here to help dedicate two Confederate soldiers' graves, both brothers in the 22nd North Carolina. We have six rifles to fire the volleys, my S.C.V. Commander Chris Washburn calling the shots. Around 100 people are here.

This 145th Anniversary of the Battle of Gettysburg starts on Thursday the 3rd of July, 2008. I drive us up to Pennsylvania and we find the event held in the same area as last year, we are just camped in a different spot this year. Lynell and I set up the tent and a staff meeting is called.

I am posted at the entrance to Longstreet's Corps as a guide sentry. Later, 2nd Lt. Underwood has me place a sign. After sitting and talking awhile, I go back on Sentry Duty. A lot of our guys start coming in. A call comes for Couriers. I am sent to check with the P.A.C.S. Commander and the Hardee's Commander on who will be going to the evening tactical. After this, I go to see if Casey Meadows had a sprayer for poison oak so I can take it to David Cooper. He didn't have it, but Barry Shephard of the Cavalry did. I clear it with Lt. Colonel Harrell, get to the Cavalry over the hill, and bring back the sprayer to David Cooper. The Major in Medical in the tent beside me needs another color bearer for the tactical. He gets me permission. We follow the troops. The Yanks have five fronts. It is a close, fast-moving fight. There are about six medical emergencies; on one, I wave my yellow flag back and forth. An all-terrain vehicle carries an Emergency Medical Services team out. At 9 P.M., I attend my first Officers Meeting as a private. I agree to be on staff at this event but not to give up my rank.

July the 4th of 2008, and here at Gettysburg, Pa., it rains this morning. We are at General Shelton's tent when the Morning Reports start coming in. Our little camp's Bonnie Blue flag is posted. The Battalion Dress Parade is finally canceled. The rain has stopped but it remains overcast which helps us out a lot. Lynell and I walk over to the Sutlers. Thousands of people are all over the place. Lynell gets a white dress hat with feathers and a green belt. I get two pencils, twelve buttons, and a Gettysburg Confederate trouser pattern. I also see Daniel Young, the Blacksmith, who tells me of the Cannon Class to be held on his farm on August the twenty fourth. Twenty-five dollars is to be paid by the fifth of August. Lynell rides the shuttle back. She fixes us a good lunch from the tent. I make a Courier trip to P.A.C.S. and Hardees Commanders. Much time for resting up and talking before the soldiers form for battle.

As we are stepping off, I am told to be a runner for General Shelton. I did a little running to get Hardees up. Longstreet Corps makes it to the big road. We watch as thousands of Confederate troops march by.

We come on and cross the road into the battlefield. The grandstands are filled with thousands of spectators. The Confederate Army comes out flanking the Federals. Then more of our troops come up on the battle line and begin crossing a stagnant, slimy, creek. I am helping the General down the bank when I see a frog looking up at the bottom of the General's foot. I'm thinking this frog is in the right place at the wrong time. After crossing, I run down the lines passing the command to put fire on the Yanks. Orders come down from overall Confederate Commander General Cornett to 'push' and 'fire'. Back at camp, I go on another Courier trip, then gather firewood.

Today is the 5th of July 2008. It is the 40th birthday of a brother-in-law, David Jones, as well as the 35th birthday of our Sergeant Major. Yesterday's battle was fought in a drizzle and it is much the same today. Practically nothing has dried out. In the tent, I shave and brush my teeth. Lynell and I cook our breakfast over the fire.

Before long, Companies and Battalions are in motion for a massive Dress Parade. As Staff Couriers, we stand behind the formation and are behind a company of reenactors from England, by the sound of them. Back at camp, 'Stinky' the Cook and another man are brought up before the General on various charges. They are taken out and 'executed' before a firing squad. One of the guys' brogans are taken off as they are carried away. I fetch a couple loads of fire wood and run off some courier duty. I bring General Shelton a couple buckets of water before bringing some to the tent of the Chief of Staff, Lieutenant Colonel Harrell. The General over Longstreet's Corps, Terry Shelton, has a couple of meetings at his tent. At one of the meetings, each Courier is assigned a Colonel to report to when sending a message from General Shelton. I am assigned to Colonel Tim Smith in 1st Battalion of Longstreet Corps.

Troops soon form for the march out to the battle. Two huge armies face each other as thousands of spectators pack the stands. Back and forth I run with messages, no rifle, just carrying a haversack and canteen. There are many medical emergencies; the battle is even stopped twice. Back at camp, Anita Harrell and her sister-in-law, Susan Hill, cook a big supper after which a musical comedy is put on.

July the 6th is our last day here at the 145th Gettysburg, and it is not raining. About 4:15 A.M., one of the 'British' men come into camp seeking help for his wife who sprained an ankle on a Porta-John trip. We get breakfast, Lynell cooks some ham. Before long, troops start gathering for the morning Dress Parade, which is switched from roadway to hillside. I am called up to General Shelton who gives me a message for ANV. Or 4th ANV. I report back to tell them when the

parade is over. It is a long Dress Parade; awards are given out including another 'Soldier of the Year' award going to another 1st Kentuckian. Allen Jackson conducts a Church Service for us in camp. I hear Sonny Bishop on bagpipes in the background. More Courier duty before the

troops start forming to go out to the battle area. I have to hunt down Hardee's Command for a message. We wait a long time before the road is clear enough of troops so we can march down by the farm house and onto the field for staging. I am one of the Couriers sent out to our Colonels at various times with messages. A horrendous cannonade goes on for quite some time. We then start advancing through the cannons, adjusting our lines on the other side. Hand held movie cameras are about, the thousands of soldiers are an awesome sight! I make it over the wall in this Pickett's Charge with no rifle.

I told a Yankee I was visiting and didn't want to go to prison. General Shelton gets a twisted ankle and a Colonel gets cut on his head with his sword. This is my 83rd event and the first in which I do not fire a rifle.

Now, it is the 23rd of August, 2008, and it is a working Saturday. I arrive in the morning at a large cow pasture where in is a graveyard. It is located south of Stuart, Va. at the intersections of routes 8 and 103. Several vehicles are already here. About 12 or 13 of us members of the Wharton-Stuart Sons of Confederate Veterans camp #1832 will be working at the graveyard at some point today. A Confederate soldier bearing the last name of Dalton being in the 24th Va. Inf. lies buried here. I am over on that knoll eight hours and there are no shade trees. I help raise the stainless steel flag pole much like the flag pole was raised on Iwo Jima. It is firmly planted at Private Willis Dalton's grave because we use three bags of quick concrete mix, rocks, and dirt filling up the hole. A Second National Confederate flag is run up, I salute it. A fence of about 180 feet long by about half that wide is put around the graveyard. We use post hole diggers and a tractor with a screw to get the wooden posts in the ground. We roll out wire fencing to fasten. On top of that, a strand of barbed wire is placed. Some people have to leave during the day. When I leave, all they have to do is hang a six-foot gate. A man is supposed to come and use a chainsaw to even the tops of the fence posts.

It is the next day, the 24th and I go to the farm of Daniel Young, the Blacksmith, at Oak Level, Virginia. I wear gray uniform trousers, leather brogans, and a rather worn long sleeve shirt. About 20 people gather here. A man and woman have come down from Pennsylvania to conduct a cannon class for cannoneers-to-be. They represent the National Civil War Artillery Association. I find out it takes three years to be a real cannoneer. Men from the Henry and Patrick County Sons of Confederate Veteran camps are here starting the process of certification. We practice the jobs servicing the cannon. The #1 and #2 men are on the sides of the tube while the #3 and #4 men are back of the wheels. The #4 man gets to pull the lanyard, firing the piece. We even have fires start down range in the grass. Daniel is a multi- talented Sutler. He and his wife have been working on making me a pair of black wool trousers from the wool I bought from him at New Market in May. He gets the pattern in exchange for making them.

On the 20th of September 2008, Lynell and I are at Chickamauga, Georgia, for what will be our only 'out west' event we will ever do. At midnight, we 'hit' Chattanooga, Tennessee, then enter the state of Georgia in our quest for the reenactment site. At the second store in which I stop to get directions, I walk up to a guy sitting in a pickup truck. Another guy comes out of the store, both of them are relic hunters. A street behind us is barricaded, he says it's probably because the Vice President of the United States may be down there; he was at the Opening Ceremonies of this 145th Anniversary of the battle of Chickamauga event. I follow one of the fellows to his house and he gives me an original Confederate bullet from the Chickamauga campaign.

We go on to register at the site at McLemore's Cove. We pull in a field by some trees and sleep about two hours in the car. We get dressed pretty much in the dark. Ladies, my wife can tell you what it's like to change into a hoop skirt in a

Chevrolet Aveo. I walk around and make contact with Captain Powell of the 47th Virginia. I salute, shake hands and talk with General Bill Russell who lets me fall in with the 47th Virginia. The 47th Va. and the 63rd Tenn. seem to be representing Longstreet's Corps at this event. We spend a lot of time at drill on the company, battalion, and division levels. Back at the camp area, a giant square is formed of the Confederate troops. Almost everyone is able to give a shout out of their Confederate ancestor and some info on him. Lynell and I tour the good amount of Sutlers. She takes a picture of H.K. Edgerton and me.

I have to be confined to camp before the battle. I rest by putting my hand on a pecan tree as I stand. We fight in a big battle, and capture two cannons and their crews. They change to our side, some put on grey. Afterwards, it's time for Lynell and me to leave. I get pictures at the Chickamauga National Park on our way out. Our Virginia General Lee license plates are well liked at the rest area.

On the 3rd Of October, 2008, I prepare for the 18th Annual J.E.B. Stuart Birthplace Encampment. After work, I drive on to Ararat here in the county. I register which costs ten dollars; the most I ever remember it being before is four dollars. I see Cpl. Brown; he directs me to camp and helps me set up the A frame tent. Others here of the 51st Va. are Captain Bobby Harris, and Private Mike Pendleton, 1st Sergeant Underwood is just arriving. Officer Terry Shelton of the 1st

Ky. Is here. I previously called my brother Judson and told him he could sleep in the tent tonight and tomorrow night. I go home and am bringing up firewood to the house when Lewis Steppe and his two sons Daniel and Zackery arrive. We get some cartridges made up.

Four of October, 2008, and we awake around 4:30 A.M. Lynell fixes us a fine breakfast but is not feeling well enough to go with us today. The rest of us leave in Lewis's Dodge truck dressed in our period attire. The sun has not come up yet when we arrive at Major General James Ewell Brown Stuart's Birthplace in Ararat, Virginia. We unload some things into the tent. At one end of our company street Roll Call is conducted then we assemble on the other end. First Sergeant Williams has me inspect the rear ranks weapons. Our Company Colors are posted. We find we are to be the Color Company for our battalion. Lewis and I are picked to be on Color Guard. The company is marched up on Laurel Hill for the Dress Parade. After this, we march to the big flagpole where the galvanized Yankees assemble also. Ronnie Haynes gets the rope unlocked and the huge 2nd National Confederate flag is raised. A cannon volley of three shots will echo and reverberate off the surrounding hills in a tribute to a passed-on Artillerist who went by the nickname of 'Cannonball.' Back at camp, Judson and I gather books that I brought from home to take to our S.C.V. table. There are about 15 Sutlers and some food vendors here. We eat food Lynell sent. The company gets in place, Stack Arms and wait. Lewis and I don't fire as we guard the flag in the battle. He goes down with a 'hit' before the battle is over. Our side wins. A stop for a fried apple pie at a food vendor before we go back to the house.

At 4:30 the next morning, we try it again prepping before leaving in Lewis's truck. Before the sun comes up, we are in the Confederate camp. Judson is sleeping in the tent. Someone has built the fire up and the flames are leaping higher than Daniel Steppe's head. There is a formation with Roll Call then Company Colors are posted. A little later, we form up again. Our company is Color Company again today. I begged off the guard for Lewis and myself so we

can 'burn some powder' today. At the same time, I put in a good word for Jud to 1st Sgt. Williams. Jud and his high school graduate friend Mike Pendleton are put in on the guard. We are marched out to Dress Parade. Chris Owens is the Adjutant. Today, Lieutenant Underwood is leaving us for a job in Texas. Our company is blessed to have had him and we wish him the best. After the parade, the Confederate Army has a professional photo taken, and individual companies have ones done as well. Travis White wears his hillbilly teeth. Allen Jackson gives a Church Call before he conducts the service at Officer Lester Harrell's tent. Preacher Alan Farley is on the hill in the big tent. Mike Pendleton gets in the shade to play his guitar and sing. We get ready for battle. The cannon firing is good, and we watch the smoke rings roll. We advance and hold our line as much firing goes on. My musket fouls out, but Judson lets me use his. Zackery and Daniel Steppe are 'Ice Angels' today.

This is the sixth day of December 2008, the Annual Christmas Parade is held in town today. Lynell and I go to Stuart to await the arrival of Sonny Spence at our parade prep spot. He comes in with his pickup and trailer that will go in the Wharton-Stuart S.C.V. Camp #1832 parade entry. We have garland to decorate the 'float,' but Lynell goes for more. Later, she goes for coffee, hot chocolate, and food for the crew. We return home and change into our 'reenacting' attire. When we return, the float has bales of hay on it. On these are put a comforter and quilts. There are eleven people on the float including Sammy Hughes's children. The camp banner, made by Jud and Mel, hangs across the back. There are over 200 parade entries. I throw a lot of candy. Once I flip a piece of candy over my head and the float and a lady sitting on the roadside caught it. A black lady calls me General. Snow falls throughout our time in the parade!

On the twelfth of December 2008, Lynell and I go to the Reynolds Homestead at Critz, Virginia, for the Annual Christmas Banquet of the Wharton-Stuart Sons of Confederate Veterans camp #1832. Dressed in our period attire, we bring in our share of the food: meatballs, corn pudding, a vegetable casserole, two pecan pies, and a soda for good measure, forgetting the yeast rolls.

CHAPTER FOUR - 2009

This is February 4, 2009, and the Annual Meeting of the 51st Va. Inf. Co. D is being held at our house this year. My youngest son Michael helps out. We go up to the church to pick up two eight ft. tables, three six ft. tables, and 40 metal folding chairs we are borrowing. In the house, tables are put in basement, den, and on main level. Lewis, Zackery, and Daniel are the first to arrive. Michael is sent to the store for gas and three bags of ice. More people start arriving. In the den the meeting of the 51st goes in session. Allen Jackson is voted in as the new 1st Sgt. Captain Bobby Harris steps down and out of the job. Lester Harrell becomes the new Captain. Twenty-eight people including women and children are here today. We have fifteen men in the den not counting Michael and his friend, Luke Underwood. We have lunch at 12 o'clock. The ladies do a fine job. Mike Pendleton comes in from the antique mall in Stuart where the celebration of J.E.B. Stuart's birthday is going on. The company votes to attend: Buchanan, New Market, White Sulphur Springs, and Cedar Creek. Brent Underwood fixes our bedroom ceiling fan lights while he is here. Lewis Steppe, Michael, Luke, and I move the tables and chairs back to the church.

This is March the 3rd of 2009 and the 51st Va. is holding its Camp of the Instruction at Laurel Hill, Ararat, Virginia. The alarm clock goes off at my house at 4:30 A.M. Lynell fixes us up with a good breakfast. Lewis Steppe and his two sons who spent the night with us, follow me over to the J.E.B. Stuart Birthplace. Yesterday, we and my youngest son Michael had enjoyed time at a nearby farm firing rifles such as a 'Winchester' Lever Action Model 94, a 22 rifle, and a 30.06 rifle. Pistols used were a .38 Special, and a .357 Magnum; also, many BBs were expended.

Over at our camp, a Roll Call is held. The 24th Va. and Captain Cooper are above us on the hill. Below in the woods are the 1st Kentucky. We all stand at Attention and salute when we see them posting Colors. In the silence, I hear a cow on a distant hill and snoring coming from our Captain's tent. We march out on the hill to be drilled in the fundamentals of marching. On returning on the break, we take a look at the basket of things Lynell had packed for us. We are back out on the drill field with our three band rifles this time. On the lunch break, we find some shade. Back on the field, we now fire our rifles. At one point, we are in a Skirmish Drill firing from the prone position and loading while laying on our backs. Later on, we break into two groups to fight in the woods. Lewis, Bremen, Terry Williams, Zackery, Daniel, and I go in first. Coming in after us are Jonathan Wilson, Mike Pendleton, Allen Jackson, 15-year-old Casey, and Captain Harrell. We have a 'shoot um up' and return to camp. Anita Harrell is cooking. Lewis and his boys have to go home. Tomorrow, Zackery will be twelve years old. The moon is nearly full tonight. There is a mock trial as the three companies have a bit of fun. I sleep under the pickup camper shell.

I awake after a night of heavy dreaming. I go to the campfire where some of the fellows are assembled. Allen is cooking in a cast iron skillet some hotdogs Mike gave him. Bremen cooks some real sausage. We have some good fellowship. First Sergeant and Chaplain Allen Jackson gives Church Call. Contingents from the 1st and 24th join us at the captain's tent fly. Allen preaches Jesus's Crucifixion and Resurrection. After Church, we have a company meeting. Ways to help the company grow are discussed. I start to leave and have a senior moment and leave my rifle. Mike Pendleton calls out to me to save the day. I'll travel up 'the mountain' to the Blue Ridge Parkway on my way to Don Lewellyn's house on the other side of Mabry's Mill on Fork Mt. Road. He invites me in to eat deer meat and rice with him. He is willing to let us have the old 24th Va. flag from the company he and I started years back. In exchange, I give him the rifle I bought off him previously for my oldest son John for $400.00. So, this is the Confederate battle flag I end up giving to the 51st Virginia.

This is April the 4th of 2009 and today I arrive in Bassett, Virginia at the 'Bassett Historical Center' to await the arrival of others. Author Tom Perry is the third person here; he will speak later inside. Members of the Stuart-Hairston S.C.V. Camp #515 begin to arrive. Daniel Young the blacksmith, sutler, cannoneer, and S.C.V. member drives up with a cannon. We all pitch in getting it unloaded and help in setting up a tent, tent fly, and flags. After the inside proceedings, four of us fire three volleys, ramming paper each time to shoot at high elevation. Mike

Wray a photographer for the 'Martinsville Bulletin' newspaper is here. Next, the cannon crew goes into action. Today, I am the powder monkey of the crew. We fire off six black powder rounds. A descendant of David Lee Ross is here. Ross was the original Captain of the 51st Va. Inf. Co. C later changed to D.

Still in April of 2009, this being the 18th and also the day we commemorate Confederate Memorial Day. I arrive at the old Patrick County Courthouse in Stuart, Va. to participate in the flag raising ceremony. As I stand at Present Arms, flags are lowered and the 2nd National Confederate flag is raised. This is performed by Larry Cassidy, Kenneth Holt, and S.C.V. Commander Chris Washburn. Mike Corns from N.C. walks up before it's over. I go back home and exchange the frock coat for a 4-button sack coat and the kepi for a slouch hat. Lynell comes to the old Courthouse with me now. She wears a shawl with her camp dress. From the front steps of the Courthouse Commander, Chris Washburn of the Wharton-Stuart Sons of Confederate Veterans camp #1832 speaks. Lynell places a Confederate flag wreath in front of the Confederate statue on the lawn. Judson is here to give the firing commands for the three volleys.

April the 24th of 2009 finds Lynell and me up at Buchanan, Virginia checking in at registration. Our 51st Va. Infantry camp is located by the James River behind the town. As we begin to unload, it was then I notice we have the old tent and the new tent poles. We make it work, sort of.

Lewis and Zackery set up beside of us. A train rumbles by on the other side of the river as Lewis looks on longingly; he works on train cars for a living. We change into period attire. Robert Brown goes with us up to the two Sutlers. We talk to Red Barbour. Lynell and I go up on Main Street. Now in camp, the fellows are setting up a fire.

Last night, we spent in the back of the pickup here at Buchanan. It is the first time for Lynell to sleep over night under the camper shell. We use the 'wrong' tent for storage. As morning comes on, we hear a few birds then the big one is heard from the rooster who starts crowing. 1st Sgt. Jackson gets me to help out on fire detail. Soon, Captain Harrell gives us a talk and Roll Call is taken. Three of us post company Colors. All of us get in on some good company drill. The company tent fly is set up behind the captain's tent overlooking the James River. Boats and canoes occasionally drift by on this warm sunny day. On the other side is the railroad and Purgatory Mountain. Having forgotten the frying pan, we eat rice medley from our cups that we set on the fire grate.

Our company forms up and marches out to a shelter to await other troops to come up. Then all of the Infantry's weapons are inspected. To opposite ends of the Field we go to await battle. Our artillery opens up and in short order a bunch of tubers come floating down the river where the cannon is pointed. After the 'saber dance,' we are called up.

We tear into the Yankees, nearly annihilating them. Captain Cooper surrenders the rest. We have a good gun cleaning time back in camp. Lynell and I go to the swinging foot bridge that we can see from camp.

This is where, in 1864, the Confederates burned the original one to deny Hunter a crossing place. In town, we eat with Robert Brown and Terry Williams. Russell from the 11ᵗʰ Va. comes up and we all go to a fifteen-room antique store. After a visit to 'Fireside Books' we return to camp.

This is April 26, 2009, and our last day of this event. Another night was spent in the back of the truck under the camper shell. After the rooster crows a few times, one of the many trains of the day come through. Later, one comes through town. Lewis explains that he is with a different company from the trains across the river. We get breakfast from the tent. A company Roll Call is taken then Company Colors are posted. Some soldiers begin drilling with the three new privates; Casey McPherson and Shawn Gilley had their first battle yesterday and

Josh Bryant has his first today. We seek the shade of the tent fly. Lewis's wife Jennifer and their other son Daniel come in. The boys amuse us as they play along the river's edge. Canoers and tubers come down the James River as Casey plays the song "Dueling Banjos" from the movie "Deliverance" on his banjo.

Our time of relaxing goes much too fast. We form up and go out to the shelter to await weapons inspection. I guess this is the first time I've ever had a Yankee inspect my rifle, a 24th Va. Galvanizer. We go to the camp to await battle which will be on the same field as yesterday. As a cannon fires toward the river, a smoke ring rolls into the trees making the leaves move. In today's battle, we are 'beat up.' We lose the Captain and Lewis; many others go down also. The Yanks push the last few of us back to our camp area. I believe I fire the last shot of the battle. I run some canteen water down my hot rifle barrel.

May 2, 2009, and I am in my Confederate uniform for the fifth Saturday in a row. As I am driving to the Reynolds Homestead in Critz, Virginia, I observe a mud turtle who is in the act of crossing five lanes of highway. Sammy Hughes has two tents and a tent fly set up at the graveyard area. On the other side of the house, Chris Washburn has his Southern Tradition's trailer set. I get a BBQ sandwich and a lemonade. The Annual 'Spring Frolic' is going on. I see Bernardo and Daisy Hernandez with their kids. Sammy Hughes, Mike Pendleton, and I fire one volley. Soon, rain sends people scurrying. Mike Pendleton plays his fiddle for music for the kids in the May Pole ceremony.

This is May 15, 2009, and Lynell and I are on our way to New Market, Virginia. We get passed on 220 North by Captain Lester Harrell in a red pickup, 1st Sgt. Jackson, the trucks owner, is riding 'shotgun'. Coming on around is Susan Hill, Anita and Bremen Harrell. On up I-81, another set of reenactors pass us on their way to New Market. These two are in the 28th Virginia, Bobby Compton with Dave Lawhorn riding 'shotgun'. It is not uncommon to see horse trailers or cannons being pulled on trailers behind pickups as we near events. We make it, set up camp, then help our neighbor Bremen a bit.

On this 16th of May, I hear a bird chirping and I get things in motion. The camp slowly begins to stir. The sausage biscuits Lynell had already made up for us are good. At this event, we have quite a few fellows 'falling in' with us. A Roll Call is conducted by 1st Sgt. Jackson. Doug Camper is in charge of a detail posting

Colors. The 51st Va. Infantry are our 1st Battalion's Color Company this weekend. A little later, we are first on the field for Dress Parade with our twenty-six being

the largest company.

I get to talk with Jeff Bower, former reenactor who is visiting. General Cornett comes out and gives us a nice speech. Greg Gallion, whose rank I am not sure of, is here also. After parade, General Shelton conducted Battalion Drill. Afterwards, Lynell and I give <u>Gettysburg at Fairfield 1996</u> DVDs that had been transferred from VHS to Officers Cornett and Gallion. We find the camp of the 28th Va. and I give Mrs. Sobataka a DVD for her husband Jeff. Later, when the 28th returns from their 2nd Battalion Dress Parade, I give Lieutenant Lawhorn his DVD. We find lunch and some shade as we wait. Our company gets an Ammo Call then a First Call.

We wait in the hot sun in formation before we move off behind the Museum through a wooded trail to wait some more. The clouds begin to thicken as the battle opens. We fire on the Yankees as they come out of the Peach Orchard. We repeatedly have to fall back and as the battle ends, lightning flashes, thunder rolls, and rain falls. Someone lost a pistol. At camp I clean my rifle. Lynell cooks steak and rice while I go to the Sutlers and buy a Georgia Infantry picture in a frame. I also go in the Bushong House.

Today is the 17th day of May 2009, and the last day of this 145th Anniversary battle of New Market. On last evening, the rain hit with a vengeance and continued most of the night. Doug Camper and his contingent, who were campaigning, left out. The New Yorkers who were being Confederates and also were sleeping out in the open got royally soaked, and are gone this morning. We have no Roll Call or posting of Colors. I sit in the tent and sew up a large opening where my black wool trousers were coming apart. Lynell cooks up a good dish of sausage, potatoes, peppers, and eggs over the fire. We attend a Battalion Dress Parade that is considerably thinner since the storm paid its visit. First Sergeant Allen Jackson conducts Church Call in our camp. Eventually we form up. It just so happens that I, at 50 years of age standing beside Travis White's 13 years old son, am asked to be on the Color Guard. On the other side is 51 years old Terry Williams. We would go throughout the battle advancing behind General Shelton and retiring behind our line before they let go a volley.

Once, a huge bang erupts as new guy Jason's rifle goes off with about four powder loads down the barrel. This happened in the real war with real loads as a soldier, in the heat of the battle, hears rifles going off and thinks his did until a cap spark breaks the blockage. After the battle we get to the vehicles then have to drive over the Interstate, through the town of New Market, to try to get close to camp. We toted out several trips then back over the Interstate and through town again.

On the 13 of June, 2009 a Living History is held at the Patrick County Museum and Library in Stuart, Virginia. We take our guests, Lewis Steppe and his two sons here for the occasion, out to breakfast first. Up the 'mountain' we all see a black bear rear up. After our breakfast at Mabry's Mill, we are coming down the mountain and a bear runs across the road in front of us to jump a guardrail. I stop, backup, look down and see a huge bear sitting staring at us. Back home,

Lewis and I change into Confederate uniforms and take Zackery and Daniel with us to the Living History.

Lynell comes by later to see us. Our group Drill, Stack Arms, March, and fire some volleys off the top of the hill. The sound of the double loads is tremendous. I think our guests had a "beary" good time.

It is the next day and after church, I am back in the uniform of a Confederate soldier. About a mile from my house at the old I.M. Akers store here in Buffalo Ridge, I meet up with Chris Washburn, Terry Williams, Lester and Bremen Harrell, Sammy Hughes and one of his sons, and Mike and Melissa Pendleton. We all follow Mike off Route 8, down Lone Ivy Road, to below Smith River Falls and below Lovers Leap to John Woods. Behind his house, one of the Confederates buried is John C. Hubbard of Co. H of the 51st Va. Infantry. Family members gather. We have a dedication for the Confederate Iron Cross that Mike Pendleton places. The crisp volleys echo into the green mountain sides. We then drive not too far away, to go behind Moir and Pansy Pendleton's old place. Here is the grave of Moir's grandfather, George Washington Pendleton. If my information is correct, he was fourteen years old when he enlisted in the 5th Va. Reserves. Cordilla Walker and her daughter Carolyn are here for this dedication as well. More good volleys are fired here.

On the 18th of June, we arrive at the house of Sean Verlik, a former reenactor, to make purchases of period clothing and equipment. This is just an example of how by keeping one's eyes and ears open, acquisitions can be made. Sometimes due to circumstances of life, people can't always fit reenacting in, this can't be held against them. We all have just been blessed to have had the opportunity. At this time, we get: A big chest, a Dutch oven, hand billows, a plate and cup, two nipple wrenches, a battle shirt, shirt, a vest, a carpet bag, two quilts, a nine-button shell jacket, bags, a nice jean cloth kepi, and trousers.

July the 4th of 2009 finds me in the park in the town of Stuart, Virginia. Along the creek in the shade trees is the encampment of the Wharton-Stuart S.C.V. Camp #1832. I help unload a cannon from the Stuart-Hairston S.C.V. Camp #515 that has arrived. Up the hill at the Patrick County Public Library, 'Confederate troops' assemble. Three men are up front with flags and five behind with rifles. Judson directs us. Behind us in the parade are lots of kids and a few adults. We Present Arms at the raising of the U.S. Flag on the park pole. The Stuart-Hairston boys out of Henry County are set up near us as is the Hunt Club. The cannon fires at 10 A.M. For the next six hours and every hour on the hour, it is fired, and I always carry the powder to the loader or #1 man on the cannon. Fifteen rounds are fired of 6, 7, and 8-ounce black powder varieties. Once, I stop the operation when a pickup is driving toward us. Chris cooks hamburgers and smokes polish sausages. A big car show goes on most of the day.

This is August 15, 2009 and I am at Saltville, Virginia. Yesterday, Lynell and I were on our way up the mountain and had truck trouble. I end up coming alone to Saltville in the car and carrying less stuff. Today is my oldest son John's 23rd birthday. He has been here in years past. Now, members of the 51st Va. awake to a pleasant morning. I have breakfast in the tent with vittles Lynell packed. Later at the Coon Hunting Club, I have a cup of coffee while Terry, Robert, and Captain Harrell eat breakfast. Jason Bryant and his parents come in camp. The Colors are posted before Sgt. Williams has us go out for a drill session. At the Sutlers, I buy cookbooks for Lynell and one book for myself on a Georgia Sharpshooter. Robert Brown and I go to the Coon Club, and I get beans and cornbread. The Hog Calling contest went on outside while we were in the club. Mike Pendleton and his wife come in. Sgt. Williams and I get in an egg toss contest which ends with egg on his vest. We spend time at the Captain's tent fly before Sgt. Williams conducts an Ammo Call. I watch salt being made; water boiled down in pots. A man with the last name of King dug the salt water wells. He sent salt on barges to his port. This is where the name Kingsport, Tenn. originates. We get ready for battle and watch as spectators come in on Smyth County school buses. We feel the repercussions from cannon fire before easing into the ongoing battle. David Cooper, wearing his havelock and with his host of galvanizers, faces us. The battle rages back and forth. Taps sound at the battles end, our uncovered heads are bowed, and I watch a spider climb onto Sgt. Williams pant leg. I pour canteen water down my hot barrel; then they want us to fight again so I take a hit. At camp, I finish cleaning the gun. Over at a blacksmith's, I listen to him tell some history. I learn today that former Longstreet Corps Commander Jim Maupin has died.

On this 16th day of August 2009, I awake here in Saltville, the saltworks of the Confederacy. Apparently, Josh Bryant slept well as I in the tent. We have breakfast here after I help Cpl. Brown get a fire going. Fog hangs over us a few hours before the sun burns it off. From time to time, I walk out things to the car. Some of us go over to the shade of a large tree for a Battle of Saltville Memorial Service. The General Lee reenactor plays a big part once drinking from a canteen and passing it around in a "we drank from the same canteen" tradition. The J.E.B. Stuart reenactor gives us an informative talk. A volley salute then taps are played. I get lunch from the tent.

Today, Tennesseans replace the men we lost yesterday. So, with our company strength of eight, we go out to a shade tree on the battlefield to wait. I see a Mountain Howitzer a few feet away start the battle. Soon, we are in a battle line and make it to a rail fence before we fire. Josh gets some of my few rounds. He goes down and soon after I fire my last round and take a horrific 'hit'. Well, later some Yahoo's are shooting big powder loads over my head so I limp over under a tree. I see some real old Confederates make a charge before I limp off the field following Bremen. We sit about breaking down camp. Thus, ends my 88th event.

It is the 23rd of August 2009 and I am the first to arrive at Daniel Young's place at Oak Level, Virginia. I wear a Confederate uniform without the jacket but with the vest. Soon, we have a few folks on hand, and I help unload a cannon off of Daniel Young's truck. He not only is a blacksmith, but can also make things out of wood such as chairs, etc. He already has a tent fly set up where we try to obtain some shade. Sammy Hughes, Chris Washburn, Sonny and Curtis Spencer, and I are here from the Patrick County S.C.V. and there are several from the Henry County camp. Soon, the National Civil War Artillery Association Cannon class begins. Larry Fischer and his wife from up North conduct the class having done so last year as well. My card expires today but I will get a new one good for two years. I serve as a powder monkey on both crews also as a number four man at some point on both. I get to pull the lanyard quite a few times, most just primers but some are powder rounds. We have hotdogs cooked by Daniel Young's helper. He is also the fireman. It rained last night so it is not too dry today. A deaf neighbor man, a neighbor lady, and a boy get to pull the lanyard as well. I give the deaf man a spent primer for a souvenir and forward one to the lady. I get several for souvenirs. I help load a cannon on a pickup.

Now it is October 2, 2009, and time for the encampment at the J.E.B. Stuart Birthplace to take place. Lynell and I arrive here in Ararat, Virginia. Corporal Brown helps me set up the tent. Lynell buys a dress, shawl, and other items from Mrs. Shirley before going back home. It has been overcast but the next two days hold promise. Now at camp, Mike Pendleton is playing his fiddle, while a friend of his plays a banjo. Brother Judson is supposed to come in tonight and stay in my tent.

Its October the 3rd 2009, and up here on Laurel Hill, last night, Judson and I slept as snug as bugs in a rug, with the quilts from Sean Verlik. I ride with 1st Sgt. Allen Jackson to park his truck. When we walk back to camp, the rest of the soldiers are drilling. Soon, we post Colors, then march out to the morning Dress Parade. A nice dog in attendance seems to enjoy all but the drums. After Parade we march out to the giant flagpole and are joined by the Yankees for the flag raising ceremony for the giant flag. After this, we see the Wharton-Stuart S.C.V. Camp #1832 setting up. Mike Pendleton and Larry Mabe come over to the big tent in the middle of the Sutlers to start playing splendidly on fiddle and banjo. Our Captain and crew all come in. Back at camp, I get the fire going again. Lynell walks up in her new hoop skirt dress. I clean rust off my rifle before we get a bottle of lemonade. Next 'door,' Judson is eating a Navajo taco at the Frybread place; we get one and join him at the next table. We talk to the guys from the Stuart-Hairston camp. Lynell is entered in a Fashion Show put on by Mrs. Shirley. I am confined to camp. We have an ammo call. At least three new men go out with us to do battle today. Our Battalion is held in reserve and gets called in at the last. The Carolina boys fight the Yankees until we come up to settle the matter. Back at camp, we clean rifles before a short Company Meeting at the Captain's tent. I walk Lynell to the Pontiac, stopping to get a cream soda refill and another look at the Sutlers on the way. I talk to a fellow wearing a bear skin; he had a bear head piece with him. Judson goes out on Guard Duty. I go out on a walk and see Judson, the Artillery camp, the waterfall, and the Boy Scout camp. I find a canteen and turn it in.

Judson and I spend another night in the tent atop Laurel Hill. The hilltop looks good with all the tents under the full moon. A crowd gathers around the company fire; it is so cold one can see his breath this morning. Corporal Brown takes two new guys to post company Colors. Again, we are marched out to morning Dress Parade, stand in 1st Sgt. Terry Williams does the honors. Afterward, the same guy that took our picture last year takes one of the Infantry. We opt out of an individual company photo this year. In camp, we find three of us are to go on Guard Duty later. Lynell comes in and we go to the main event tent over on Sutler row. Evangelist Alan Farley of Reenactors Missions for Christ conducts the service; at least five people are saved. Afterwards, I wait to get the autograph of J.E.B. Stuart's great granddaughter but she keeps talking to the Evangelist. I get to talking to Mike Corns and his friend Rob from Lawsonville, North Carolina. I take Rob over to talk to Lester as he may seek to join our unit. I cook some rice medley and Lynell and I eat. Eventually we accouter up to go out and stage for battle. We sing 'Dixie' as the Yankees go by. Down in the woods, we go. As leaves drift down, cannons boom in the distance. Our line goes forward, fires a good bit, and falls back as the Yanks are behind the breastworks. We shift twice and are firing when I run out of ammo and take a 'hit.' The battle rages on and we win. I look behind me and see Judson stretched out. Cpl. Brown fell a few feet away. The only two Cavalry men I saw all weekend ride by.

It is now October 16, 2009, and wife Lynell and I are headed up to the 145th Anniversary Battle of Cedar Creek, Virginia. Off I-81 on the Middletown exit, we are almost immediately at registration. Captain Harrell and his crew are here at the table. We follow them on in. At this event, we receive a medallion with a blue and gray ribbon we are to have with us at all times.

We help Allen, Terry, Bremen, and Susan set up their tents before we set up ours. I help Bremen and John Lee on a wood detail. Our soldiers are tying in with the 1st Ky. this weekend. At the Sutlers, Lynell gets a hat and collar. I get another rifle nipple and a book called 'The Unwritten South.'

This is Saturday the 17th of October, 2009, and we are up at 4 A.M. on the original battlefield. We make a break for the 'little houses'. On returning, Lynell has a coughing spell. She goes out to sit by the fire that I build up. The 1st Ky. have a Roll Call then post their Colors shortly afterward. We get breakfast from the tent. I get ready for Dress Parade early but get up with our combined company late. This is the only Corp event of the year. After parade, all of Longstreet Corp marches out in the open. Here Sgt. Henry Kidd tells us of a discovery in California made in 1937 of a recording of the real Rebel Yell as performed by a J.E.B. Stuart Cavalryman. He demonstrated it and its three parts. The sounds are like yeeee, whoop, yhoowlll!

I go to the Sutlers and get beeswax candles, a bag of peppermint tea, and a tea basket. We start to cook and that's when my stint on Guard Duty begins. General Cornett comes out and greets me by name as he knows me from our 28th Va. days together. He then mounts his horse to ride off with some of his staff. Back at camp, we have good soup and sandwiches after I got some ammo. The rain, that started after I got to the tent from Guard Duty, continues as the Corp assembles for battle. For the first time, I see an 'Ice Angel' pouring hot chocolate. Two cups of it are passed throughout the company as we wait and wait. We hear the booms of cannon and then we advance with our lungs giving out the newly revived Rebel Yell. As we cross a creek, a soldier jumps and falls before I jump and I land near him. On up the hill, he takes a 'hit' because of the pain in his arm from the creek crossing fall. A Medical Emergency occurs, the battle is stopped, and E.M.T.'s move in. We pass in Review. I clean my rifle and cut off a piece of hanging shoe leather. Over the fire grate, we cook rice medley, steak, peppers, and onions. I get firewood and water.

This is our last day here at the 145th Anniversary of the Cedar Creek Event. Sometime during the night, the cold rain stops falling on us. I sleep with three pairs of socks on plus jean cloth trousers, a shirt, vest, wool and jean cloth lined jackets, a night cap, and kepi. Covers consist of at least five layers of blanket and quilt combinations. With a candle for heat and some spooning, we make do on the air mattress. We start, as each reenacting day starts, with a trip to the Porta-Johns. We have some breakfast, try to get warm around the fire, and have no Roll Call or posting of Colors. Robert Brown comes walking up wanting some breakfast.

The Corp goes out for Dress Parade. We are greeted by the sight of Captain Harrell and Colonel Shelton holding hands and skipping out to join us. I don't make this stuff up, folks. The 8th Virginians are celebrating their 40th year as a reenacting company and 25th year in Longstreet Corps. The Soldier of the Year Awards for the Infantry and Artillery cannot be handed to either because neither of them is present. After the Parade, we informally gather around and some tell stories and memories of General Maufin, our Second Corp Commander. Now he and our First Commander, General Hillsman, have passed on. We enjoy some leftover heated beef stew and biscuit bread around a smoky fire. More of our men come in camp to join us. Allen Jackson holds our company Church Service. Yesterday, Allen, Terry, John Lee, Bremen, and I fell in with the 1st Ky. On this day, the 51st takes the field as a company with Robert, Mike, Larry, and Jason all coming in. After the 'hurry up and wait' in which all our rifles are in one stack, we march over near the 'Heater House' to engage the Yanks. This starts a series of hasty withdrawals which involve a lot of confusion and some firing. The battle is stopped for a Medical Emergency as yesterday. I forgot to bring the truck key. I change in the tent then get it. Lynell has everything packed we get out okay.

This is October 24, 2009, and I participate in a Grave Marker Dedication ceremony. First, I drive to the home of Mike Pendleton. He takes Larry Mabe and me to the site out at Ridgeway, Virginia, south on 220, and off of road number 689. We come out of some woods to then go into a graveyard surrounded by them. Here lays the final resting place of 2nd Lt. Thomas Alan Price of the 45th N.C. who died of typhoid fever. There are ten of us in uniform, six with rifles, three with flags, and a sergeant also with a rifle to call it. Family members, as well as members of the Rockingham Rangers, Stuart-Hairston, Wharton-Stuart Sons of Confederate Veterans are present. The sun came out as the ceremony to dedicate the new marble headstone gets underway. Afterwards we see other graves out in the woods. Mike gets us back.

It is November 7, 2009, and last night, I arrived here at Ft. Branch, North Carolina, and was able to get in as a 'walk on' for $15.00. I slept in the truck, and this morning, the camper shell is encased in frost. I dress in Verlik's old outfit and with rifle and accouterments, cross the road to the Confederate camp to search out a suitable company to fall in with that would have me. I join with the 20th N.C. As I watch, they commence to cook breakfast and invite me to join them. At first, I refuse, then accept. Over the fire is bacon, sausage, potatoes, mushrooms, and about two dozen eggs cooked together with seasoning. We form up to go out onto the field in front of the Fort. My file partner carries an original 1845 3 band musket that was dug up at Jacksonville, North Carolina. At the Battalion formation, Henry Kidd is here to educate us on the Rebel Yell. We have a lot of Company and Battalion Drill.

I go to the Sutlers and get a muslin cloth bag and some rounds. I see a 'dressed out' deer being butchered for the meal they are having tonight. Back at camp, the fellows are rolling rounds. I buy a pound of black powder from them. I go to the Museum where old cannons from the earthen fort are located. I talk to Henry Kidd about the Rebel Yell. The first two parts of it are short and the last part long. I walk around inside the Fort and view the deep river below the 70 feet tall bluffs. Back in camp, I see the 20th N.C. cook has just put the main part of a pig on a spit to roast over the fire. We Stack Arms and wait in two different places before the battle. I see smoke then hear the opening cannon shot. It is a bad battle as they make us fall back before a smaller force of Yankees.

I enjoy coming and reconnecting with Ft. Branch for this 16th Anniversary of my time reenacting. The road leading out is lined with fields of cotton. I remember my dad telling of days when in his youth, he picked cotton from sun up to sun down. There were 14 children in his family, 12 lived to adulthood.

At the annual Christmas Parade, we attend and participate in Stuart, Virginia. I prepare by putting on black wool trousers, brogans, gray frock coat, belt, gloves, and a black derby hat.

Lynell has on a camp skirt, with a shawl and straw hat. At the Church lot across from Moody Funeral Home, we meet members of the Wharton-Stuart Sons of Confederate Veterans Camp #1832. They have a red pickup with a trailer attached with hay bales on that. Two of the camp banners adorn the sides. We talk to Terry Williams. Ten people ride the float with two in the truck. On this cold, cloudy day, we toss candy to the kids. Going down Main Street, I see my brother David with his wife Terri and one of his sons, Daniel. Many are the firetrucks, cars, floats, etc. in this parade. After the parade, we talk to Lester Harrell and some of his family members. About halfway back to the parade starting point, one of the trailer tires goes flat.

CHAPTER 5 - 2010

On January 16, 2010, we travel to Lexington, Virginia, to celebrate Confederate Generals Lee and Jackson who both at some time lived here and made contributions of their time in institutions of learning here. We park at the Visitor's Center and walk up to the cemetery on the hill top where Lieutenant General Thomas 'Stonewall' Jackson is buried. A crowd surrounds his statue.

This part of the proceedings is about to end as wreaths have been placed. Some soldiers fire a volley. I take a few pictures. I left my rifle with Lynell, who is well photographed sitting on her wooden stool. Where the people are gathering for a parade, we see Cpl. Brown of the 51st who immediately invites us in. We are marching through town when Mike and Melissa Pendleton, Larry Mabe, and Scott Hylton join in. I'd say there is a few hundred of us. We march to the V.M.I. Parade Deck.

More pictures are taken, then a walk over to Lee Chapel on the campus of Washington and Lee University. As I still have my rifle, we just stay outside. Inside is singing, a guest speaker, etc. The Public Broadcasting System is filming the event. The camera is turned on Lynell and me for an

interview; Lynell does most of the talking. I walk over to get the car and drive back. We go to the museum where the stuffed hide of Stonewall's horse, Little Sorrel, is located. Also housed here is the rain slicker the general was wearing when he was shot.

A redhead with a rifle, was well photographed.

This is February 13, 2010, the day this year's meeting of the 51st Va. Infantry is held. It is at the fellowship hall of the Patrick Springs Providence Methodist Church. The meeting was to be held at our house on the 6th J.E.B. Stuart's birthday but was snowed out. Even on this day, there is still plenty of snow as some fell last night. Lewis and Daniel, one of his sons, are our guests and will go to the meeting with us. Before we all go to the meeting, the food gets loaded up. It includes chicken casserole, vegetable casserole, meatballs and wieners, rolls, mixed nuts, relish tray, potato salad, two pecan pies, and a 2-liter drink. The fellowship hall is nice. Others bring food for the meal to be held after the meeting. Don Lewellyn comes in; he is one of the people that started the 51st but has been away a few years. There is eighteen of us present including women and children. Lester Harrell, whose house is in sight of this place, goes back in as our Captain. We have seven, really eight, events scheduled with two more being questionable and a Camp of the Instruction place is still to be announced.

Lynell and I are on site for the 145th Anniversary of the battle of Bentonville, North Carolina, on March the 20th, 2010, having arrived last evening. It takes us a long time to get set up deep in the woods.

Buglers from various points across the encampment ring in the first day of spring. First Sergeant Jackson has a fire going which I take care of while he moves his vehicle. After a walk in the gray dawn, I happen upon a clean 'sink.' At camp, we get ready to roll out as other units march by. I speak with Junior Switzer as we were in the 28th Va. together. We assemble on the road and march to the field beside the Sutlers to experience the first taste of what leaves a bad taste in our mouths today, waiting.

We wait for this big weapons' inspection to be conducted by North Carolina rules. Well, when it finally happens, they don't touch our weapons. They only watch as the rifles are inspected but not primed and capped off. Earlier on this field, we had a Dress Parade. Immediately after, Captain Lester Harrell led us in some Company Drill. Lynell and I go to the many Sutlers who have good selections. We purchase a candle of the beeswax variety, a small box of matches, a collar of the type she has long looked for, and a belt. We eat sandwiches in the tent.

Again, the time for us to do something has changed. When I get back in camp from the 'sinks', the company is already accoutered up. As we are about to march up the path, our spirits are lifted as Pvt. Travis White, his two sons, and a daughter come in. Now, our company has twelve in all.

 On the path/road, we wait once again as spectators, Cavalry, and Infantry clog it up. We march over near reenactor parking to a huge field where periods of silent waiting are punctuated by brief firing until the battle finally explodes. Our entire company is wiped out. I lay near our Captain and General. I hear General Shelton snore as we wait once again. At camp we clean rifles. I go to take pictures including one of the Joe Johnston statue.

 Here at Bentonville, N.C. we sleep good on the air mattress loaned to us from Mike and Mellissa Pendleton, they now have two cots. After our usual morning walk, we cook over the fire on the fire grate. Our fare is potatoes, bacon, peppers, eggs, and bagels. Anita Harrell cooks more food than anyone else. Well, I pull out the fake plastic hand I bought yesterday and try to get Travis White to believe I had had plastic surgery done in West Virginia.

He gets his daughter Hannah to video me talking about it. This weekend, we get to hear Mike on the fiddle and Larry on the banjo; they are well photographed and videoed. I help in posting Company Colors.

We march out to the field between the Sutlers and the new Joe Johnston statue. We join hundreds of other Confederate soldiers to get the same kind of Weapons Inspection as yesterday.

During the long waiting period, I take pictures and shake General Cornett's hand as he comes up to me. I see Private John Hutton who has been reenacting since 1960 or so; his ancestor and mine were in the same unit.

Back at camp, I carry a couple of loads of bedding and stuff to the pickup on the other side of the Yankee camp. In camp, a Church Service is conducted by Allen Jackson and Travis White.

I take out another load of stuff before we eat. I have to accouter up and go out and wait. Our company has Privates Pendleton, Mabe, Wells, LeViner, Thomas, and two with the last name of White; Corporals Brown, Williams; Sergeants Harrell, Jackson; and Captain Harrell present for both battles both days and we all 'take hits.' Our grand moment comes when we come out of the woods and overrun a Yankee breast works. I personally 'shot and butted' a Yankee. Later, we are caught between two Yankee lines.

Today is April 10, 2010, and some of us go up to commemorate the 145th Anniversary battle of Waynesboro, Virginia, where nearly all of the 51st Virginia were captured near the end of the War. I wear my Confederate uniform and take my rifle and accouterments to Patrick Springs to Lester Harrell's house before 5 A.M. Temperatures are in the thirties. We wait for Terry Williams to drive in and change into his uniform. Bremen Harrell joins us as his dad will drive us all to Bassett Forks where we meet Allen Jackson and Scott Hylton. Scott drives us in a van to Waynesboro, Virginia, where he then changes into some Confederate clothes. Now, on the phone with Robert Brown, he guides us in and we arrive just behind him.

This first reenactment site is located outside of town on land someone let us use. I fill a few canteens with water. The older Private Bryant joins us. The younger, his son, is not here. First Sergeant Jackson has us do some drill. We have only a few minutes to grab some food before boarding a Fishburne Military Academy school bus for a ride into town where the real battle is fought. The Cook 'Stinky' in the next picture is also a Gentleman.

We unload, then march to a graveyard to step over the fence as no one has a key. We participate in a Memorial service by firing volleys over the graves of soldiers.

Officer and friend Bill Russell

The Plumb House is below.

We tour the Plumb house, see bullet holes from the battle, and also see a lady born and raised there, before taking the ride back. John Lee Thompson and his Mom come in; I get her to take some pictures for me in the upcoming battle. Our Confederate force is about 25 including two runners. We also have Chuck Carter, his crew, and a big cannon. The Yanks have a small cannon. Their cavalry and troops close in upon our breastworks. I disobeyed a Lieutenant Colonel and the Yankees by refusing to surrender. Before we leave, I buy two Confederate memoir books.

Today is April the 17th of 2010, and we are having our Confederate Memorial Day observance here in Patrick County, Virginia. Our Wharton-Stuart Sons of Confederate Veterans Camp #1832 Commander Larry Cassidy opens the proceedings. A member of the camp, Steve, leads us in prayer. High school history teacher and our camp's 1st Lt. Commander, Shannon Brown, gives a good speech. Some 1400 Patrick Countians served, if I am hearing him correctly. I am in the Honor Guard. We stand behind the Statue of the Confederate Soldier on the old courthouse lawn. Four of us, including two from the Henry County Camp, fire volleys as my brother Judson calls the shots. Many pictures are taken.

This is April 23, 2010, and Lynell and I arrive at Buchanan, Virginia, to check in at the registration. There are no parking passes, event passes, or set of rules handed out. We set up our tent down by the James River. In the middle of the night, a train comes barreling down the track on the other side of the river. I actually think it is coming through our tent. Before day light, we make a Porta-John visit. This is the first one I have ever seen with a hand washing station inside. Some soldiers get a fire going and I take some pictures. Terry Williams, John Lee Thompson, Jason (last name not known), and Robert Brown post the Colors of the 51st and 60th Virginia.

We are called out to drill by 1st Sgt. Jackson. As previously instructed by our captain, we all have a little fun at Jackson's expense as all drill orders are not executed properly. Earlier, Mike Pendleton and Larry Mabe came in and set up.

Sgt. Williams marches John, Robert, Larry, Mike, and me up on Main Street. On up from us, some S.C.V. members, are in a Memorial Service at a monument. On a back street, we meet up with the captain and the 1st Sergeant. Lynell takes a picture of me holding a rooster who crowed at me at bayonet point.

We stage on Main Street and soon a battle erupts. We exchange gunfire with Yankee infantry and cavalry. The cavalry gets close and I stick my tongue out at one. I Stack Arms in front of Ransoms Drug Store. Some eat here and some of us go back to camp. We clean our rifles. I buy some ammo from Mike Broome of the 1st Kentucky. I take a picture of the 28th Va. Captain Sonny Bishop and Eric Bowers posing with their Highland Bagpipes.

We have a Dress Parade then a Weapons Inspection before marching out along the James River to the battle site. Soon flames of fire are leaping from four places in the woods. We commence to give the Yankees a good 'thrashing'. Once, when we are encircled by Yankee Cavalry, a horse brushed against me.

Back at camp, we clean rifles and Judson drives up in his big white pickup truck. Lynell and I take pictures on the swinging foot bridge. Before the free meal, Jud and I have our picture taken with 'Red' Barbour.

This is April 25, 2010, and during the night, rain, as well as a couple of tents fell. When the tent of Terry Williams fell, he spent the rest of the night in a shuttle bus for canoeists. Judson spent the night under my camper shell and reports a leak.

In camp, we have Roll Call, then I carry the flag as we post Colors. Lynell cooks breakfast over the fire as another one of the trains comes through. The Captain is still in his tent but comes out by Church Call. Judson attends the pavilion church service held by Rev. Alan Farley. Allen Jackson holds a church service in our camp complete with communion. Later, a memorial service is held for the "dead" John Lee Thompson. It is said Captain Harrell gave him a heart attack.

Judson has his own drill manual here with him. He adds to it the 'Copper Top Rest.' The 28th Va. come by doing the 'Craig Mt. Creep'.

We get accoutered up and are joined by Doug Camper and his men. First Sergeant Jackson runs us through some drill that includes 'Guyandotte British Stepping'. More troops come out and we have a Weapons Inspection. Back along the river, we march to stage for battle. Judson and I have a good conversation with the current 28th Va. 1st Sergeant Dave Sutton. A while after the 28th has been on the battlefield, we come out to join them on the battle line. We advance toward the Yanks, taking 'hits' as we go.

I take a 'hit' not knowing Terry Williams has just gone down behind me. I trip over his rifle. John Lee steps back and then steps on my rifle. As we are leaving the field, a big rain fell. Before we get back to camp, the sun shines a bit. We try to let the tent dry out some before taking it down. Fincastle Rifles Camp # 1326 S.C.V. Commander Red Barbour is flanked by Jud and myself.

This is May 22, 2010, and last night Lynell and I arrived here at Spotsylvania, Virginia, via the 'Wilderness'. Last night was also the first night at a reenactment that I slept on a cot, and this is my 95th event. So far, our 51st soldiers here are Allen Jackson, John Lee Thompson, Mike Pendleton, Robert Brown, and me. I sit recalling how, on last night, I went to Headquarters to give Junior Switzer a copy of the '96 DVD of Gettysburg at Fairfield and found out he is in a battle with cancer. General Cornett said he would personally get it to him. Also, I gave Captain Shelton of the 1st Kentucky a book on the Orphan Brigade that I had purchased in Athens, Georgia.

This morning, I show a photo of the 28th Va. at the 135th Sharpsburg to the 28th here now. The 51st Va. members fall in with the 1st Kentucky. The Bryants come in and go to camp to set their tent up beside of ours. There is a Dress

Parade complete with a lengthy Officers' Meeting.

After the parade, we have extensive Battalion Drill. Captain Harrell and his son Bremen come in for the last of the drill. In camp, I Stack Arms, then have lunch from the tent. I find Leland Hedrick of the 28th who was in the afore mentioned photo. Today, the 51st Virginia takes the field as a company, there are ten of us including the Captain. A Battalion Weapons Inspection is held. General Cornett gives us a rousing speech before we march out. We are instructed to dig trenches and build breast works.

Our lines send out several cannon volleys. I not only see a smoke ring from one of the cannons, but also from one of the guns of the dismounted cavalry skirmishing out front. In the battle under the direction of Captain Harrell, we pour fire into the Yankees. Back in camp, we clean rifles as spectators with cameras stroll through. Today, I take several pictures as well. Lynell heats up some M.R.E. food over the fire as the first rain of the day comes in. We eat in the tent. We have a Company Meeting before the Captain and Bremen leave going back. I shave, then get caps at one of the few Sutlers.

During the night, thunder shakes my cot; there are brilliant flashes of lightning and heavy downpours as well. In the morning, we have breakfast in the tent. I take out a load of bedding to the truck and Corporal Brown helps me with another load. We soon accouter up and go out for Dress Parade. Allen Jackson is a Lieutenant and Terry Williams is moved to the 1st Sergeant's position. Lynell takes some pictures. Back in camp, Terry helps me with another load going to the truck. Around 10 A.M., Allen Jackson conducts an in-camp church service.

Lynell and I move more things out to the pickup in the parking lot. Ardie, a new recruit, is learning drill movements He has been in the U.S.M.C. for over 20 years. He has been in Recon, been a Parris Island Drill Instructor, and been in several war zones.

Hundreds of motorcycles roar by on the nearby highway. Reenactors line the hillside and wave their hats. Earlier, I had signed a card that was going to Junior Switzer; now, we wait about camp.

A signal gunshot is fired and the camp springs into action. Before I can fire a shot, we capture a company of Yankees. We fire a bit, then recross the creek. Amid much confusion and firing, we get the best of the Yanks. At the farthest point of advance, I take a 'hit,' then take some pictures. This is the first battle for Ardie and he survives. General Cornett gives us more uplifting words and we give him three cheers. In next photo, John Lee Thompson takes aim.

I change clothes in the tent before taking it down. The Bryants help us out. We drive to Waynesboro and find the Cracker Barrell with Mike and Melissa Pendleton inside. At this event, we camped next to them, and our vehicle was parked next to theirs.

On June 19, 2010, this year's Covered Bridge Festival is held once again. I attend a church meeting so I arrive later in the day. Judson and Lynell had set up

our tents earlier near the Jack's Creek Covered Bridge. The Wharton-Stuart Sons of Confederate Veterans Camp # 1832 of which Jud and I are members has a tent fly set up. A couple of wagons drawn by mule and horse teams carry people back and forth for the Bob White Covered Bridge not too far away. It is hot and Lynell is a real trooper for staying with us in her period attire. We talk with a few folks. Across the road, vendors are set up and live music is playing.

On June 26, 2010, Camp of the Instruction is being held at the J.E.B. Stuart Birthplace also in Patrick County, Virginia. When I arrive here in Ararat near the North Carolina state line, I see Terry and Robert moving about. Some eight or so tents are set up as some stayed here last night. Before long, 1st Sgt. Allen Jackson conducts Roll Call. Robert, Terry, and I are the Color detail and post Colors. The guys get breakfast. I ate breakfast before I left the house. John Lee Thompson drives about ten miles to his house to eat breakfast and will do the same for lunch. When we assemble for drill on this hot, sunny day, it is without coats or rifles. Two new guys, at least to us, are here, Ardie and Skip. Skip Fletcher has plenty of reenacting experience and comes to us having moved up from Florida. Captain Lester Harrell and the 1st Sergeant see that we get plenty of drill in. Mike and Larry are here as is Ardie's little girl. After, a time, Chuck Carter comes in to join us. We gather at the slave graveyard in the shade to talk and rest. Later on, we get lunch; I have food I brought from the house. In the shade on a trail, we practice Stacking Arms and rifle drill. It is time for a tactical fight. The Captain will be unarmed and act as a referee. He has Ardie, Terry, Mike and me go out first and the rest to come find us. I set up in a spot across a field with my back to the Ararat River and shoot every one of their team eventually. Going back, we are the aggressors, and Ardie and I have a field day. We are never 'shot' except but by people who have already been 'shot.' Mrs. Anita, Bremen, Miss Lil, and Mrs. Susan are in camp. Mrs. Anita gives a class concerning women. I drive home where Lynell is preparing our Wedding Anniversary meal.

On July 9, 2010, I drive into the Reynolds Homestead with Judson's tent that I picked up from our mother's house (Doris Ward LeViner Smith). About eight A-frame tents plus the Captain's Wall tent are already up. Sammy Hughes and his two sons help me set up two tents. I unload period clothes. People start coming in for this year's 51st Virginia Infantry Company D's Camp for kids. We have ten kids and eight adults present. I march the kids to get firewood. I start a fire and heat up some food. Bremen Harrell marches the kids to the building for video viewing.

This is the morning of July 10, 2010, and last night the crew all slept in the Activities Building. I slept in the back of my pickup truck. Some rain fell during the night.

I enter the building and take pictures of a snoring Sammy. We are talking outside when Lisa Martin, Program Director, drives up to fix breakfast for all who are awake by now. The kids return their sleeping bags to camp. I start a fire from last night's embers. After water is heated, I use it in cleaning my rifle. The kids, at least some of the bigger ones, train with muskets. Sammy is in next picture.

Sergeant Harrell puts them through the 'Paces.' Judson LeViner and Mike Pendleton come in to join Bremen Harrell and me in firing muskets as instructed by Officer Sammy Hughes.

The cannon crew from Henry County comes in and sets up. The kids are drilled with and without weapons. Earlier, a big, black snake made for a good picture with Sammy Hughes pointing my musket at it.

We all pose for photos around the cannon. After a break, a cannon crew is mustered to fire two shots, a 6-ounce and an 8-ounce shot, of black powder. Ethan Hughes issues gear, Jud is the powder monkey, I am in the 1 position, a Henry Countian is on 2,

Sammy is on 3, Capt. Harrell is on 4 and pulls the lanyard as commanded by Daniel Young.

After another break, the kids are taught the 'Guard Against Cavalry' drill. Around the big, brick house, the kids are marched and drilled. Allen Jackson is kept busy entertaining a young lady from Ararat who is helping us out. At one point, they are dancing. We march to the Rock Springs; some students from Virginia Tech are here. Today, they have worked in the slave graveyard. We go to the building for lunch. Not long after, the captain and 1st Sergeant leave out. Sammy rigs up some cane poles for fishing. The children fish in the ponds out back and I take pictures that I will get developed and bring back to Sammy.

July 11, 2010, I have arrived back on site seeing only one person at a little after 6 A.M. Last night, they stayed in their tents. The guy is Alan Bouldin, a plumber and fellow S.C.V. member. We walk over to Sammy's pickup where we enjoy a free beverage from his cooler. Mr. Bouldin and Sammy's son, Ethan, load up a couple of rifles and fire outside the tent of 2nd Sgt. Bremen Harrell. The camp is awake now.

Down at the building, breakfast is served by yet a different lady than yesterday. Sammy shows me the kids' folders, they have pictures from yesterday in them; also, that were taken after lunch when the cannon was fired four times before it went back with Mr. Young. Mike Pendleton comes in to help with the kids today. They march with rifles a bit and then they are allowed to play 'Capture the Flag'. Parents start arriving. Lester and Anita Harrell arrive in civilian attire. Sergeant Harrell marches us out to perform drill movements with the rifles.

Lieutenant Sammy Hughes hands out folders to the parents and addresses the crowd on hand. The kids are marched over to the camp to return rifles and period clothing. I show some parents my maimed hand because a child found it fascinating, they like the fake hand I show, too. Mike Pendleton and I take down a good number of tents.

The evening of August 27, 2010, I arrive at Elkton, Virginia, for a reenactment. I see no registration signs but I see Terry, Allen, and Bremen. Cpl. Brown helps me set up my tent. I talk to Red Barbour and Ardie. During the night I dream a mama bear and two cubs are chasing me; I spend a good part of the night trying to hide and look out for them.

On the morning of August 28, 2010, Ardie gets a fire going.

He along with Cpl. Brown and me post Colors. 1st Sgt., for now, Jackson conducts a Roll Call. I walk to the registration tent to still go unregistered as no one is here. I go back to camp and read from the book <u>General Lee's Army</u>. Then, Terry and I go back and get our passes as we are preregistered. At camp, we get accoutered up along with members of the 11th Va. We practice mostly Skirmish Drill. Allen, Terry, Robert, Bremen, Ardie, and I go out. We see Mike and Larry come in. Back at camp, John Lee drives up with Captain Harrell and Mrs. Anita in tow. We help them unload, then all of us get lunch here at the camp. Ardie prepares a big meal for his family that come in.

Around 1 P.M., 2nd Sgt. Harrell conducts an Ammo Call. We head out to the battle through a wooded trail and a lone black snake crosses in front of us. We stage in the rear of four cannons. Eleven of us deploy as skirmishers and the twelve of us stay back. Some Yankee cavalry show up. Some of the skirmishers go over to camp and change-over to be Yanks. We are thrown into battle, then it stops. A cavalry man has a can of powder flame up on him. We have a black cavalryman on our side. At camp, we clean rifles. I now go to the Sutlers in search of buttons, needle, thread, and a soda; but I find none of the above. We hear of an upcoming meal that our passes can be used to obtain. On my way to get supper, I walk back over the battlefield and find twenty-five good

cartridges to go with the three good caps I found earlier. We enjoy the pork, green beans, slaw, desert, and lemonade. I find three more rounds. At camp, Captain Harrell holds 'court.' Katherine is one of the people on trial. In one 'trial,' a man ends up getting 'shot' by his wife.

This the morning of August 29, 2010, and we are still at Elkin; quite a few trains ran somewhere close by during the night. In the morning light, we begin stirring about and later, the captain arises. I walk across the battlefield to the Community Center where the Boy Scouts are hosting a breakfast to raise money. I have coffee, eggs, sausage, biscuits, and gravy. Back at camp, Colors are posted and others are cooking breakfast. Mrs. Anita Harrell cooks enough for a company, as usual. Ardie is cooking again as he will do again later on. I take a load of stuff out to the pickup then read some. Chaplain Allen Jackson holds Church Call. We meet under and near the captain's tent fly. We have preaching, praying, and singing. I take more things out to the pickup.

We eventually get accoutered up, go out, and Stack Arms. One of Ardie's boys, Chase I believe is his name, will be our flag bearer again today. This is his brother Hunter's first event with a rifle, and he does very well. I lose the cork to my canteen and use a piece of cedar wood to plug it. The four cannons go off, the sabers rattle, and we are on a skirmish.

Their cavalry never gets close to us. We spot a galvanizing Chuck Carter and send some fire his way. Everyone has a good time.

This is October 1, 2010, and tonight, Lynell and I arrive at Ararat, Virginia, at the birthplace of Major General J.E.B. Stuart, Cavalryman of the Confederate States of America. We register, find our camp, and set up our tent with the assistance of Cpl. Brown. Judson arrives, also.

The next morning, by the light of a fingernail moon, I get my canteen filled with water from a spigot. First Sergeant Bremen Harrell conducts Roll Call and oversees posting of Company Colors. We assemble to march to the large flagpole on Laurel Hill. Finally, we stop marching around and stand at Attention. Henry Kidd walks out of his Historic Gallery Sutlery and buttons up his uniform jacket. As he salutes, I Present Arms and can see him past the second band of my 3-band musket. A giant 2nd National Confederate flag is raised and then lowered to half-mast. We have Battalion and then Company Drill.

Back at camp, I give Colonel, I believe that is his rank, Gallion a couple of pictures. Lynell and I go to the Sutlers. I get a jean cloth block I military vest and get my picture taken with Henry Kidd.

We make some other purchases, then share a Navajo taco and lemonade for lunch. We wait until we get back to camp to share the fried apple pie we bought from a local vender. I sew another patch on my 4-button sack coat. Allen Jackson's parents bring in chicken and banana pudding! Lynell gets a dress from someone in camp for twenty dollars. I sew a button on my shirt while I am still wearing it. Soon, we are marching off to stage for battle. The cavalry engages in battle; then we face cannon fire. Cpl. Brown, Jud, John Lee, and others go down. I find myself now guarding the Colors as we move closer to the enemy. Then as a horrific boom sounds out, I look skyward and see a large smoke ring floating over me. I fire into the center of it as I kneel over backwards.

Another brother of Jud's and mine, David, comes by. This is his 46th birthday.

This is also the 20th Annual event here and Jud has attended them all. We have Guard Duty tonight from eight to ten.

This is the morning of October 3, 2010. The predawn day starts out as did yesterday. Several of our 51st Va. members go out on various duties. Mrs. Anita

Harrell is busy cooking bacon in a large frying pan. Timmy Ring confesses to Captain Harrell that he called him fat, but says John Lee Thompson 'walked him into it'. Company Colors are posted then retrieved a little later as we take the field at Dress Parade of what remains of Longstreet's Corp. David Cooper is called front and center and it is stated that this is his last event. He is captain of the 24th Va. and is in a Yankee unit when they galvanize to provide Yanks for us to fight. He has been reenacting since 1986.

Later at camp, a church service is conducted by Rev. Travis White.

He suffered a leg injury in yesterday's battle, but he preaches well today. Lynell and I go up the hill as we are camped in the low field near the highway. I take pictures of Evangelist Alan Farley.

We pick up some lunch. From the camp, I go to the truck and get a pair of brogans for Patrick Wells who has come in to wear so that he can fight in the battle.

After an Ammo Call, we take the field, have a Weapons Inspection, march to the back side of the top of the hill, and are posted in the woods. Our second rank comes out in front of our cavalry to lay hidden in the prone position.

We ambush the Yankee cavalry and, then, let our cavalry have what is left of them. Our company now in the woods experience a lull in the battle. We come out and 'hammer' the Yanks. It is David Cooper's last stand. I shake his hand and thank him for all he has done over the years. Terry Williams and I exchange some shoes. Lynell and I take the long way home.

This is October 16, 2010, and last night Terry Williams helped Lynell and me set up our tent here at the Cedar Creek Battlefield in the top part of Virginia. We slept rather well.

A predawn inspection of the Porta-Johns is made by Lynell and myself. As the day is dawning, I help set up the fire grate. Other privates go on a water run. I take some pictures as well as deliver some. I give some photos to the 47th and 28th Virginia Units as well as some to our company. Up at the camp of the 1st Kentucky, I buy powder and caps off of Mike Broome. Lynell and I have breakfast in the tent.

We get accoutered up and go out for Dress Parade. We are addressed by General Cornett and Colonel Gallion. Junior Switzer, on staff, is back from his bout with cancer. After parade, I shake his hand. We have a Weapons Inspection before being marched around by Officer Bill Russell and then have a short fierce battle with the Yankees.

At camp, we clean rifles. Lynell and I go to the Sutlers of which there are many. She already has bought a $25 cape in camp and now buys a dress. North State Haberdashery put on heel plates and hob nails, bought at Fall Creek Sutlery, on the soles of my brogans. Lynell gets us lunch from the fry bread place.

Before long, we are accoutered up again. Colonel Russell commands our Brigade which is under Shelton which is under Cornett. The battle is slow to start. We cross over a creek, then we have to fall back over and over again; finally, I fall down to keep from having to do it again.

Back at camp, we have a rifle cleaning session. The wind blew horrifically last night and today. Lynell is cooking supper over the company fire. I pull guard duty at Headquarters from six to seven o'clock. Overall Confederate Commander General Cornett shakes my hand and thanks me for some pictures I had sent to him.

Today is October 17, 2010, and during the night here at Cedar Creek the wind died down some. Lynell cooks up some breakfast over the company fire. She starts out helping me carry a load of stuff on my cot to the car but Terry Williams steps out helping me carry it the rest of the way. We have a Dress Parade; scholarships from Longstreet's Corps are handed out. One goes to the son of 28th Va. member Chris Caveness. Chris is a lawyer and his son will be studying law at Harvard. Lynell and I carry two loads each to the car parked across the road in a big lot. It's a long way and when we get back, Allen Jackson is just ending the church service with prayer. It is noted by Sergeant Major Jackson the prolific use of tobacco this weekend by John Lee Thompson. Apparently, his mother does not know about his cigars and snuff. Down at the end of our company street, beside our tent, Captain Harrell conducts a company meeting. Upcoming events will include some 150's is discussed. Lynell puts out some sandwiches she made earlier for our lunch.

Soon on this sunny pleasant day, we get accoutered up for battle. I bring along the camera to take a number of photos. Troops from A.N.V., P.A.C.S., and Longstreet's Corps start amassing.

After some marching about, our company is placed between the hubs of cannons on the firing line. The elder Mr. Bryant is on the crew of the one on our right. Our company, the 51st Virginia Infantry, is Color Company and I stand back guarding the flag until the captain gets me to firing. Colonel Russell gets us in close to the Yanks. It is hard work and he gets a drink of water from Mike Pendleton's canteen.

After the battle, Lynell and I leave for home. On the way, we stop by Bell Grove Plantation.

It is November 5, 2010, and Lynell and I encounter snow on our way to Guyandotte, West Virginia. In the V.F.W. Building, we find Corporal Brown eating tacos. He helps us set up our tent and soon we are at the corner pizza parlor. Back in camp, Captain Harrell's crew are delighted with the huge pizza box I have purchased. When on the box is written, 'It's Guyandotte, Baby!' and a photo taken, we now have put this event into proper perspective.

This night is the first time in seventeen years of reenacting that I use a heater in the tent other than a candle. Before we left for the event, we borrowed a 'Mr. Heater Buddy' from Sammy Hughes. We also found out that they lied when they said there would be 24/7 indoor facilities and coffee.

On the morning of November 5, 2010, we file into the V.F.W. Building across the street for breakfast. H.K. Edgerton of Ashville, N.C. comes in and we have our pictures taken with our Confederate battle flag toting friend.

Back at camp, I tote up some more firewood. Cpl. Brown, Private 'Cupcake', and I post Colors. I get to carry our Confederate battle flag to post and salute it. Lynell and I go to the Sutlers. I get a white haversack and a pair of suspenders. The first haversack I had was a white canvas one, but over the years, it has about worn out. I am thinking about the early war look for the start of the upcoming 150th Anniversary events.

When we get back, the 'King and Queen' of Guyandotte, Terry and Joan Williams, are setting up and settling in. I go to the Sutlers with Sonny and Betty Spence. Sonny and I get a pair of 'gators' a piece. They are leggings that are mostly used for ceremonial purposes now a days. At the First Guyandotte Baptist Church, our free lunch consists of soup, cornbread, brownie, and a drink.

We go out for a Weapons Inspection and then to battle. Brandy joins us for her first battle.

After a cannonade, we advance firing on the

Yanks. H.K. Edgerton is waving the Confederate battle flag, taunting the Bluecoats.

At camp, I see Pete Camper, Doug's dad. I used to be in the 28th Virginia with them. Practically all of us go to Linda's to eat, a favorite restaurant of our first 51st Captain Jerry Aldhizer. H.K. and friends are already here. Afterward, Lynell and I join Joan, Terry, and Robert at a candle light service. There is a big-time dance in the V.F.W. Hall where some, like John Lee aka Private Cupcake, dance.

This is November 7,2010, and time falls back an hour during the night. A heavy frost lays on the ground and water is frozen in the buckets here at Guyandotte. We go across the street to eat breakfast in the V.F.W. Building. Our camp Colors are not posted today. Lynell and I go back to the tent with the 'Mr. Heater Buddy' and take a nap. I hear some commotion and see preparations for a Memorial Service. We join most of our camp in the First Guyandotte Baptist Church where Stan Claridy plays and sings, as he also does later out on the street.

Later on, the street in front of the V.F.W. Building, H.K. Edgerton gives his rendition from memory of Michael R. Bradley's poem, "I Am Their Flag'. As the black gentleman in Confederate uniform holds a Confederate battle flag and speaks out, I take pictures and wipe tears.

I Am Their Flag

I Am Their Flag

Their mothers, wives, and sweethearts took scissors and thimbles, needles and thread, and from silk or cotton or calico-whatever was the best they had-even from the fabric of their wedding dresses, they cut my pieces and stitched my seams.

I Am Their Flag

On Courthouse lawns, in picnic groves, at train stations across the South the men mustered and the women placed me in their hands. 'Fight hard, win if possible, come back if you can; but, above all, maintain your honor. Here is your symbol,' they said.

I Am Their Flag

They flocked to the training grounds and the drill fields. They felt the wrenching sadness of leaving home. They endured sickness, loneliness, boredom, bad food, and poor quarters. They looked to me for inspiration.

I Am Their Flag

I was at Sumter when they began in jubilation. I was at Big Bethel when the infantry fired its first volley. I smelled the gun smoke along Bull Run in Virginia and at Belmont along the Mississippi. I was in the debacle at Fort Donelson; I led Jackson up the Valley. For seven days I flapped in the turgid air of the James River bottoms as McClellan ran from before Richmond. Sidney Johnston died for me at Shiloh as would thousands of others whose graves are marked 'Sine Nomine,'-without a name-unknown.

I Am Their Flag

With ammunition gone they defended me along the railroad bed at Manassas by throwing rocks. I saw the fields run red with blood at Sharpsburg. Brave men carried me across Doctor's Creek at Perryville. I saw the blue bodies cover Marye's Heights at Fredricksburg and the gray-ones fall like leaves in the Round Forest at Stones River.

I Am Their Flag

I was a shroud for the body of Stonewall after Chancellorsville. Men ate rats and mule meat to keep me flying over Vicksburg. I tramped across the wheat field with Kemper and Armistead and Garnet at Gettysburg. I know the thrill of victory, the misery of defeat, the bloody cost of both.

I Am Their Flag

When Longstreet broke the line at Chickamauga, I was in the lead. I was the last off Lookout Mountain. Men died to recue me at Missionary Ridge. I was singed by the wildfire that burned to death the wounded in the Wilderness. I was shot to tatters in the Bloody Angle at Spotsylvania. I was in it all from Dalton to Peachtree Creek and no worse place did I ever see than Kennesaw and New Hope Church. They planted me over the trenches at Petersburg and there I stayed for many long months.

I Am Their Flag

I was rolled in blood at Franklin. I was stiff with ice at Nashville. Many good men bade me farewell at Saylor's Creek. When the end came at Appomattox, when the last Johnny Reb left Durham Station, many of them carried fragments of my fabric hidden on their bodies.

I Am Their Flag

In the hard years of so-called 'Reconstruction' in the difficulty and despair of years that slowly passed, the veterans, their wives and sons and daughters, they loved me. They kept alive the tales of valor and the legends of bravery. They passed them on to the grandchildren and they to their children, and so they were passed to you.

I Am Their Flag

I have shrouded the bodies of heroes, I have been laved with the blood of martyrs, I am enshrined in the hearts of millions, living and dead. Salute me with affection and reverence. Keep undying devotion in your hearts. I am history. I am heritage not hate. I am the inspiration of valor from the past. I, I Am Their Flag.

In camp, Allen Jackson conducts a church service for those people present.

Brandy is not only a good soldier, but a good singer as well. After the service, we make our way over to the V.F.W. Building for another free meal. I speak with Steve Musser, he was my former S.C.V. Commander of the camp I helped start in Hillsville, Virginia.

Our company gets hurried up so we can wait. We get put on assignment and help other Confederates escort Yankee prisoners down the street. We are now back to our starting point and waiting again before cannons open the battle. We fight Yankees here on Main Street, nearly exhausting our ammo. I end this year's reenacting lying in the street with my head between the yellow lines and a leg propped up on Doug Camper's foot.

This is December 4, 2010, the day for this year's Stuart Christmas Parade. Lynell and I arrive at the Primitive Baptist Church lot where our parade entry

assembles. A few folks are here, and others come in including Sonny Spence pulling a trailer with hay bales to sit on. Brother David, who lives here in Stuart, is walking by with his son Daniel Leviner. I give him my camera to take pictures of us when we come down Main Street. Lester Harrell, our 51st Va. Captain, and 1st

Sgt. Allen Jackson are here to take charge of the troops in our entry. Curtis Spence and I, in our Confederate uniforms, are up front wearing the 'gators' purchased at Guyandotte and carrying between us the Wharton-Stuart Sons of Confederate Veterans Camp #1832 banner. Some ladies march behind the men. Lynell is one who rides on the trailer.

We have about 25 people in our entry. After the parade, some of us are getting a ride back to the starting point on the back of the pickup John Lee Thompson is driving. He nearly slings off Lester, but Terry saves the day by holding on to our Captain. Snow falls throughout the parade and a picture David takes makes it into the <u>Confederate Veteran</u> magazine, eventually.

After the parade, the 51st get together for a time of food and fellowship in Patrick Springs at the home of Lester and Anita Harrell.

On December 18, 2010, Lynell and I are in our 1860's attire once again. We are at the Rotary Building in Stuart, Virginia, representing the Wharton-Stuart Sons of Confederate Veterans Camp #1832, as we greet persons arriving for this month's meeting of the Patrick County Music Association. Later, I take food to the Reynold's Homestead as Lynell and I attend this year's Christmas Banquet for the S.C.V. I sell six of the CDs of the 51st Va. reenacting in 2010, and also my 51st year on Earth. The proceeds all go to the Company of the 51st.

Chapter 6 - 2011

This is February 5, 2011, and time for the Annual Meeting of the 51st Virginia Infantry Company D. Earlier on this day, we are at the antique store in Stuart, Virginia, where a birthday celebration for the town's namesake is going on. Here we see Marvin and Shirley Keene, Mike Pendleton, Kenneth Holt, and fellow 1977 high school graduate, Ronnie Haynes. Tomorrow is the actual date of Major General James Ewell Brown Stuart's birthday. We have some cake and Lynell even buys an antique China cabinet before we leave. Back home, we load up with food to carry to Patrick Springs to the Providence United Methodist Church for the 51st meeting. There are around 30 people present. Captain Harrell, Sgt. Jackson, and treasurer Mike Pendleton go back in at their positions. We vote on events. Events scheduled are Waynesboro, Buchanan, Spotsylvania, Manassas 150th Anniversary will be a big event for this year. I sell a few more CDs of pictures of our 2010 reenacting season.

This is April 1, 2011, and Lynell and I have arrived here at Waynesboro, Virginia. Skip Fletcher is the only 51st Va. member we see, and he helps us set up our tent. By the flickering light from the dying candle in the lantern hanging on our A-frame tent, I transfer my remaining layers of cover over onto Lynell who is trying out a new cot. I am warm and cozy in the camouflage sleeping bag on my cot.

As the day begins to dawn, we see frost lying about. 1st Sgt. Jackson is out by the dog bone fire pits I had placed wood on during the night. Soon, the funnel cake truck drives up to set up across the fence and is joined by a B.B.Q. outfit. So much for Sutler row. People set about getting breakfast and Colors are posted. They are near our tent as it is the last one on the Company Street. I set a frying pan of sausage on the fire grate and park the pickup at a nearby elementary school. We have a Company Drill and those of us who were not at the Camp of Instruction, see new things being done. Doug Camper walks in after drill is over. Later, I see Mike Pendleton in for what is left of the day. He speaks of seeing rain in Buchanan. A few minutes later, I see Terry and Joan Williams in camp. Some soldiers are sent to dig trenches. I spot a blacksmith set up off by himself in the creek bottom. I buy two tent stakes and a two-hook hanger. It is made to straddle a ridge pole and one hook is longer than the other. This is the first one the blacksmith has ever made at this, his first ever 'Civil War' event.

We get accoutered up and our rifles get inspected. We are enduring winds greater than I saw in March. We march out to be hit by snow pellets. We fight the Yankees from our trench. Once, I am one of the skirmishers that is called out. As they try to surround us, I run with the flagbearer as some of us escape. Thus, ends my 100th event.

This is April 29, 2011, and I arrive at Buchanan, Virginia alone as Lynell has to do school-teacher work. I see Chuck Carter. No 51st Va. member is in camp; a 28th Va. member helps me set up. As I walk to the tent at night, I see muzzle

blasts from a gun battle in the field.

Cpl. Robert Brown enjoys a quiet moment in camp.

In my tent, having no watch, I get up to get dressed and hear the resident rooster crow. I got out of the habit of wearing a wrist-watch years ago so as to not have a non-period wrist tan line. Birds tweet as I step out into the night to inspect the facilities. The Big Dipper is over Purgatory Mountain on the other side of a full flowing James River. Soon after the first of the trains of the day come roaring through, I hear some snoring coming from the captain's tent. 1st Sgt. Jackson is using an Irish accent today. I fill some canteens with water, buy a wooden $40.00 camp chair, and greet Mr. Lawhorn of the 28th Virginia. Our camp has a Roll Call and posts Colors. I help Cpl. Brown, Pvt. Pendleton, and Sgt. Williams set up their tents as they come in to camp. The company does some drilling. I go to see Mr. Young, the blacksmith, to do Martinsville registration and see my son Michael and his girlfriend Rebecca. We look around a bit, then my company is called up for action.

I advance up past the Bank of Botetourt to Main Street where we engage some Yankee Cavalry. At one point, a saber hit my upturned rifle. Near the end of the battle, John Lee runs out on the street to manhandle a Yankee off into captivity.

After the fight, Michael, Rebecca, and I eat at the soda fountain sandwich shop on Main Street. Allen Jackson keeps us entertained for quite a while. Back at camp, I clean my rifle before Michael and Rebecca have to leave. Later on, the troops assemble to march to the other end of town. Red Barbour is the announcer for this year's battle once again. I had a black cartridge put in my box by the 1st Sergeant as did three other soldiers of our company. I draw mine first and take a 'hit,' so it is a one-shot battle for me. Later, fire trucks come by as black smoke rises in the distance. We then have a free meal.

Up on Main Street at the Trinity Episcopal Church, I sit in my Confederate uniform to hear, along with a packed crowd, Dr. James I. Robertson speak on the subject of 'Test of Faith: Religion in the Civil War.' The distinguished Virginia Tech History Professor has authored or edited more than twenty books including <u>Stonewall Jackson: The Man, the Soldier, the Legend</u> of which I have an autographed copy. He is a fellow Danville, Virginia native. This coming Wednesday, he will retire after 42 years of teaching. He is fond of trains, I hear; as he is leaving the podium, I see behind him out of the windows a train passing by the back of the church. I remember him leaving us with the words of an unknown Confederate soldier. Those words are powerful and I have them framed and hanging on my living room wall. Those words follow here:

I asked God for strength, that I might achieve,

I was made weak, that I might learn humbly to obey.

I asked for health, that I might do greater things,

I was given infirmity that I might do better things.

I asked for riches, that I might be happy,

I was given poverty, that I might be wise.

I asked for power that I might have the praise of men,

I was given weakness, that I might feel the need of God.

I asked for all things, that I might enjoy life,

I was given life, that I might enjoy all things.

I got nothing I asked for – but everything I had hoped for.

Almost despite myself, my unspoken prayers were answered.

I am among all men most richly blessed.

This is May 1, 2011, and considering the train that rumbled down the tracks on the other side of the river in the middle of the night, I still had a good night's sleep. Things are a little slow to get going today. We have a Roll Call with our rifles and then they are inspected. Later, a Color Guard is put together to post Colors. Hannah carries a rifle with fixed bayonet in search of her brother Sam and John Lee, overdue from a water run. Her father, George, looks on as she starts off. 1st Kentucky members are playing baseball and soon some 51st youth join in. James is interested in one of their girls. I talk to Red Barbour for a while; I am also taking items from the tent to the truck. Light rain comes and goes. Larry Mabe comes in and now the music begins in earnest. Larry is on banjo, Mike plays the fiddle, and Bobby of the 28th Va. is on wooden spoons and singing. Later, Allen Jackson has church at the captain's tent fly. The rain stops before we march to the other end of town to do battle with the Yankees. I survive the whole battle and give Russell, doing duty as a Yankee today, a hand up. Before we march back, Terry Williams has a momentary relapse and runs over to a pen of chickens. I'd say chicken thieving must be a hard thing to overcome.

This is now May, 20, 2011, and Lynell and I have arrived at Spotsylvania, Virginia, to get registered. I find Skip and his tent. Lynell and I set up our tent, then Skip and I go to park our vehicles. Cpl. Brown drives up. I help him and Sgt. Shifty, aka Terry Williams, set up. Captain Harrell and others are here, too.

This is the morning of May 21, 2011, and we enjoyed a good night's sleep on our cots in our tent. One of the three buglers is sounding as I have a pan of sausage on the fire. Lynell has breakfast in bed again. I lay down and get caught off guard. I have to scramble for First Call. We are inspected, then have to wait for the Yankees to get out of their camp. We leave and march through our last year's camp site. Over past one big Sutler, the Corps is halted on an asphalt road. Runners of various ages run by as we applaud, the last being a 3 year old girl. Now we fire at least two volleys before Police block the four-lane road for our two battalions of Confederates to cross. We make a sweep through the woods only encountering a few Yankees and I don't fire a shot. A few of us rest behind a log and I munch on hardtack and beef jerky which Skip had handed out earlier. Back across and we come upon a stuck ambulance. We regroup and back into the woods we go. After more creek crossings, we hem in some Yankee Cavalry. We take off again and overrun some Yank Infantry. Esther Davis, our flagbearer, begins feeling funny. Capt. Harrell and 1st Sgt. Jackson sees that she gets medical help. She drinks water and water is poured on her head. Terry Williams reports a copperhead snake sighting.

At camp, we clean rifles and seek shade under the captain's fly. Several of our men are called out on Guard Duty. Lester and Esther return from the Fredricksburg hospital. We form for a Dress Parade. The Corp's insurance is addressed. I am called out front and center and recognized for my recent completion of my 100th event milestone. General Cornett shakes my hand. Many of these events came, I know, when he was my captain.

I am on my way later to a large Confederate Cemetery to take pictures at Captain Harrell's request, when I unexpectedly top a hill to see General Cornett and his whole staff looking right my way as they are posing for a picture another photographer will take. To this day, I regret not being bold enough to take the photo I had unexpectedly come upon.

At camp, I help Lynell cook supper. Judge Terry Shelton holds court. 'Shifty' Williams is court martialed for being responsible for the captain's chair falling off of a supply wagon to its destruction. A 'pig' witness does a good job at the trial. I am a guard and we march him to Headquarters where Officer Gallion 'shoots' him with a pistol. For some offense, Allen Jackson is ordered to be 'shot'. The Sergeant tasked with the job said, "He was harder than a tick to kill."

This is May 22, 2011, and this morning in the tent I find a tick on my stomach. We eat the breakfast I heat over the fire. There is a Roll Call and then 1st Sgt. Jackson also oversees posting of Colors. First Call comes and we march out to a big Dress Parade. Yesterday, I stood by our flag representing 1st Battalion. Today, we are not Color Company. Later, Church Call is conducted by Allen Jackson. The Chaplain, Lynell, and I have lunch. Hundreds of motorcycles roar by as a helicopter flies overhead.

We accouter up, get inspected, then march over to the site of last year's battle. Trenches have been dug on either end. After we 'hit' our trenches, horsemen clash and cannons roar. Privates John Lee Thompson and Sam Davis have footwear submerged in mud. We brace for an attack. The final push of the

Yanks comes to our right at the 1st Kentucky. We see the Yanks going back across the field with a Confederate Battle flag. Captain Harrell orders us to take the flag. I sprint through Bluecoats to tackle the flagbearer! Captain Harrell moves fast for a big guy, and his son Bremen is just off my right shoulder. I happen to be the first there and just gave a flying tackle. I pounce on the flag and can hear the roar of the crowd being glad it is taken back. It then takes only a second to realize what is going on. Their Captain turns back to utter a load curse word and declares it is their flag. He and my Captain engage in verbal combat as I slip off back to our lines at Shoulder Arms. The 'Bluecoats' were the 44th Va. galvanizers reenacting the capture of their flag from the real Battle of Spotsylvania. No one told us. Anyway, I heard Officer Shelton thought the whole thing took about eleven seconds which it probably did. General Cornett said, "It looked real!" the nice long rip in the back of my patched, butternut colored, four-button sack coat I get from the tackle only adds to my late war impression.

This is Saturday, May 28, 2011, and I arrive in my Confederate uniform just below the old Courthouse in Rocky Mount, Virginia, for Confederate Memorial Day. I meet up with Terry Williams, Skip Fletcher, Robert Brown, and Pete and Doug Camper. Doug is in charge of the troops. Some of the 60th Va. are here as well as a 2nd Va. cavalry member. We are single file at the Courthouse where pledges, prayer, and speeches are made, wreathes laid, and our three volleys are fired. Cpl. Brown's wife and son, Kevin, are here. Kevin takes pictures and video with my camera. We follow Skip to his house in the country. His wife Beverly is here. She and Skip prepare food and we all have much fellowship also. They have a magnificent house with a peaceful view. Some of us leave after the meal. The Browns are going by Virginia Tech where their daughter will be attending.

June 18, 2011, is a very eventful day for me. My oldest son John is visiting with his wife, Anna. John and I go to the home of Captain Harrell, we just missed Ardie being there by about five minutes. I pick up items he had borrowed and brought back: my vest, black wool trousers, and butternut jacket; I only went there to pick up my canteen. The captain gives me a newsletter. Back home, we take our wives over to have a look see at the Covered Bridge Festival going on at the two covered bridges at Woolwine, Virginia. We observe two horse drawn wagons crossing through the Bob white Covered Bridge. I remember when it was still a public road and driving through it myself. Back home, John and I clean rifles. My grandson, Oron, is brought in by his mother, Valerie, for his first visit to Granddaddy's house. We have a good visit and pictures are taken on this grand occasion. All too soon, John, Anna, Lynell, and I have to leave out. We travel to the Smith River Sports Complex. On the back side is where the 'Battle of Martinsville' Reenactment occurs.

John and I fall in with Officer Doug Camper and the 60th Virginia. We both deploy as skirmishers and are 'killed.' Allen Jackson fights with the 1st Kentucky. Skip Fletcher is a Yankee today. Lester and Bremen are spectators. I fail to see one horse, and this was an April 8, 1865 Cavalry battle.

This is July 15, 2011, and time for the Va. Inf. Co. D's Camp for Kids. In my Confederate attire, I travel toward the Reynolds Homestead but stop at the Captain's house in Patrick Springs to talk with Sammy Hughes, Chris Washburn, and Mrs. Anita before traveling on. I unload some items, then walk around and rest. Sammy drives in and helps me set up my tent to go with the four others already here. More people come in and more tents pop up.

Period clothing is issued. I instruct the troops in marching before we eat supper.

This is the morning of July 16, 2011, and from the bed of my pickup where I slept under the camper shell, I saw the full moon briefly. During the night, it began to rain. Sammy slept in his truck also. The kids are aroused from their waterproof tents and marched off to breakfast in the Activities Center. Chris Washburn and a helper who works here have breakfast ready. Afterwards, Chris gives one of the best presentations I have ever heard on reasons for the 'War Between the States,' Lincoln's unconstitutional acts, etc. the different Confederate flags are presented and explained. Sons of Confederate Veterans' Commander Sammy Hughes also speaks and presents artifacts. Bremen Harrell marches the kids, twelve in all, back to camp and instructs them in drill. I fire several loads of black powder with my rifle for the kids to observe. I help unload the cannon that has come in from the Henry County S.C.V. Camp #515 with men to help fire it. I am the #3 man as we fire the cannon twice.

I leave out and take my mom to Christiansburg to see her great-grandson Oron for the first time. A bunch of us eat supper and have a good time.

This is July 17, 2011, and I arrive at the Reynolds Homestead in Critz, Virginia before 6:30 A.M. I pull in beside Sammy's truck behind the graveyard. His windows are part way down as he lays snoring in the front seat. Only when I open my door does he awaken, so therefore, I cannot take his picture as I planned. Chris Washburn uses a triangle to awaken the camp for breakfast. Dreama Foley helped wake some. I hear stories about the guard duty of last night. Chris got bobcat and bear sounds to come out of his I-Pod. Sgt. Harrell marches the kids down for more sausage biscuits, etc. at the Continuing Education Center. Mike Pendleton comes in and we get sixteen chairs out before light rain hits. The twelve boys are marched out by Sgt. Harrell in the rain before their parents. Captain Hughes hands out a certificate to each young soldier. I take home some period clothes. I will return later to take down the tent, giving it time to dry out. Five other A-frames are still here drying.

This is July 22, 2011, and I pick up my brother Judson from his home on Pintail Lane in Franklin County, Virginia. Close by, we wait to meet Mike and Melissa Pendleton to follow them as we all head for the 150th Anniversary of the Battle of 1st Manassas or 1st Bull Run. Judson rides 'shotgun' as we travel to the biggest event of the year. At registration, he gets in on Lynell's ticket, she opted not to come due to the heat. We receive black wrist bands. A line of traffic coming in is held up by some people talking to each other. It's around 3 P.M. when we arrive in unbelievable heat. I see Lester Harrell; he is the 3rd Brigade Commander in Longstreet's Corp at this event. Allen Jackson helps Jud and me set up our tent. Some are already set up and others are arriving. We help some fellows from Utah set up a tent fly across from our Captain for this event, Bremen Harrell. Jud goes with me to park the truck far away near perhaps the biggest power line I have ever seen. We take pictures. Huge bleachers are set up. There are large, air-conditioned tents. A truck is set up at one end of Sutler Row spraying a cooling mist. As the evening cools ever so slightly, some units even have drill. We are encouraged not to get in uniform until tomorrow due to the heat. Corporal Brown inspects Judson's and my rifles.

It is because of this fine gentleman, Robert Brown, that you are able to be here with us. He gave me a journal as a Christmas gift because he enjoyed reading some of my journaling. I determined to use it to write more extensively on the upcoming 150th Anniversary events.

Skip Fletcher and his wife come by. I give him some pictures from the Memorial Service at Rocky Mount, Virginia. Earlier, I gave pictures to Terry Williams who is here with his wife, Joan, and to Cpl. Brown as well. Many of us sign a petition giving our support to General Cornett when he next faces the Gettysburg event organizers. General Cornett has our best interests in mind. Joan Williams is responsible for the cooling clothes we can wear around our necks. I eat in the tent. The heat at night is horrific! Doug Camper and crew come in after dark to tie in on the end of the street. Judson finally comes into the tent and gets some sleep. He tried to sleep on the bleachers but the emergency vehicles kept waking him up with their lights and noise.

This is the morning of July 23, 2011. A drummer comes through the camps as we get an early start. Captain Bremen Harrell sends me down to Headquarters for assignment. Provost Mike Pendleton has me to go get the number of bayonets in each company of the 3rd Brigade. The 60th Va. is present at the Roll Call of the 51st Virginia. Judson's new canteen leaks and he will return it later for another one. Our company is mostly wearing the green battle shirts with white trim made for 'early war', or early war impression. We march out and join hundreds of troops and then march on to join thousands. We end up at a stand of trees out in the middle of a field. The real battle today is with the heat. I hear one man dies before the battle begins. It is one of the hottest, sweatiest days of my life so far. We Ground Arms, then in the shade, we await the coming battle. Water and ice are passed out. Ice is free here but costs $4.00 a bag in camp. Travis White is 2nd Sergeant for this event and has one of his sons on the field. The cannons and the horsemen have fun before we do. We are marching when I see the first infantry volley. The Louisiana Tigers with Henry Kidd join in marching across our front. We soon open fire on some distant Yanks. We fire by volleys and at will. We slowly and in an orderly fashion start to fall back. I pull the straps of Cpl. Brown who is my file partner. I can hear Officer Harrell who is commanding our 3rd Brigade of Longstreet's Corp. All this time, the battle is going on over in front of the packed grandstands. Soldiers on both sides sometimes have on the same type uniforms as red shirts, or blue shirts, etc. I personally have on a blue kepi. We get back to the hill where we entered the battlefield and the whole battle is halted for a break. I see two black Confederate soldiers in our ranks today, who I am glad to reenact with.

Judson is talking to our ole friend from the 28th Virginia, Chris Caveness, who is a lawyer. We are talking about bears. He says that last week he was in Wyoming observing a grizzly bear teaching her cubs to chase elk. Thousands cram the stands. I hear later the price of tickets is $75.00 for adults and $50.00 for children. The announcer is good and gives out good history on various units represented. Officer Lester Harrell is taken away due to the heat. Due to some units having limited firing time before the break, General Cornett has us go back to camp. The General calls both Judson and me by name as we march back. I take off my kepi to him. Weapons are cleared and cleaned, at least mine is. The battle rages on long after we are back. In the tent, I lose my battle with the heat. The sports drink, water, ice, wet rags, all fail. At one point, I take off the battle shirt and ring out the sweat. Jud first seeks out a spot of shade behind the tent, then places a shelter half over the camp chair he has disassembled to make shade. He now has enough shade to get his head under. I hand him ice, at times. Finally, I move to a strip of woods below camp where some others are. I snooze a little on two rocks, all the good spots are taken. Rest slowly helps, plus sipping water from my canteen. The loungers jest at people who are passing by. Judson and I come up with a plan. He drives the pickup in camp as we have seen others driving in. We load the pickup and leave a few of his things here, before going to park under the huge powerline in the big parking lot for a little shade. I try to cool down with ice. Using the daylight left, I read from the book Robert E. Lee's Civil War. A few yards over, I go to a tent and get a free sports drink and water. One reenactor walks up and gets three free chicken dinners: one for his wife, one for his child, and one for him.

This is July 24, 2011, and at the midnight hour, I am rudely awakened from my pallet underneath my pickup truck. Bright car lights shine in my face from a few feet away as one of the thousands of cars out here cranks up. I get more sleep then get up around 5 A.M. as the traffic noise increases, mostly Emergency vehicles, police cars, and horse trailers. I start getting ready, then Judson shows up while it is still dark from camp. He brought in his cooler. I really enjoy the ice from mine. The heat is staying with us today. I put the tent ridge pole under the truck and close the back down. Into camp we march, I am only carrying my rifle and accoutrements. The Bryants are already here having arrived from their motel stay. I repay them $5 for the ammo I obtained from them on the field yesterday. Jud and I lay on the spot where our tent once stood. A fingernail moon is high overhead in the breaking day. Low flying jet liners leave vapor trails. We take some 'clowning around' pictures.

Ever so slowly, the camp comes to life. George Davis is here with his wife and kids and one of their cousins. They really add to the company. Down on the road, we are preparing to form up as a company. Melissa Pendleton is using my camera as I want a picture of us in our battle shirts. She also gets a picture of Jud holding a bayonet at Terry's behind as he is getting water at a water station.

Longstreet's Corp is all here now. The Louisiana fighting Tigers cannot wait to get to the battlefield and start a fight amongst themselves. Bill Edwards of the Tigers, at least for this event, is called Front and Center for what is one of the highlights of this 150th event. I remember him from the first event I participated in. He is presented with two awards, one by General Cornett. He used to be Captain of the 12th Virginia but stepped aside to let someone else take that position. Now, he is proclaimed Captain once again. This event was the first one for Mr. Edwards fifty years ago. The Corp is highly motivated and cheers loudly.

We march out to the battlefield to stage at the same tree line as yesterday. We Stack Arms and break ranks. Dave Sutton and Bobby Compton of the 28th Va. prop up against stacked bags of ice. One reenactor gets his picture taken with kids and slick talks the ladies. Travis white and I sit and talk. Soon, we unstack arms and march out. After we have engaged the Yankee hoards a while, the Louisiana Tigers come by our front, then we resume firing.

The same thing as yesterday, shoot and fall back. I pull my file partner Cpl. Brown back, then he goes down and I run out of ammo. Lieutenant Harrell has me get some of Cpl. Brown's ammo. Later, I see Cpl. Brown back in the ranks. I shoot caps sometimes. I run out of ammo again as I am desperately trying to fight my way back closer to the parking lot. 1st Sgt. Williams gives me a few rounds. Maybe at some point, the Confederates beat the Yanks as, I believe, they did 150 years ago. Back to the hill of yesterday, the break comes. I clear my weapon and Jud and I are released to go. On the dirt road just coming to the battlefield are hundreds of fresh confederate troops. Judson and I are some of the first ones to get out of the parking lot. Mike Pendleton helps me with information concerning the 3rd Brigade of Longstreet's Corp. Companies present at one point were: 18th Virginia Companies B and G, 51st Virginia Company D, 1st and 6th Kentucky, 63rd Tennessee, and 28th Virginia Company C.

This is September 17, 2011, and on last evening, Lynell and I arrived here at the Lake Watch Plantation for the Franklin County Civil War Days. I shook hands with Commander Greg Gallion before we set up the tent. Being up early today, I venture up the hill in search of breakfast. It soon arrives from Bojangles via a pickup truck of the Fincastle Rifles S.C.V. Camp #1326. I have a sausage and egg biscuit with coffee and take Lynell a bacon and egg biscuit. The free breakfast is nice. Red Barbour gives out black powder to those of us who were preregistered. Judson slept on the ground out in the open last night and falls in with the 28th Va. this morning for Roll Call. The 51st Va. has a Roll Call with rifles. Afterward, I clean on my rifle. Lynell leaves to go home, speaking to General Lee and Traveler on her way out. The three-starred Overall Confederate Commander spends a good deal of time talking to Jud, others, and me. There is an Officers' Meeting 'next door' as I find I am camped behind Headquarters. Judson makes a path to the camp of the 28th through some bushes. Now, banjo music rings out from Headquarters. The rest of George Davis's folks come in. Bremen Harrell shows up and is our Officer-in-Charge. Tomorrow, Captain Harrell is supposed to be here.

Judson busts up some firewood for 'Stinky' the cook for Headquarters. We go out to drill that includes Guard Against Cavalry as horses encircle us. After Mike Pendleton and Larry Mabe come in, we accouter up for battle. I see smoke then hear the cannon that fired. Smoke rings fly as the battle rages. Jud, then I take a 'hit.' Lieutenant Harrell and 1st Sgt. Jackson and what is left of the 51st, 60th, and 28th Virginia push forward to victory!

Back at camp, we clean rifles. Sam Tucker of the 18th Va. was with us on the field as well today. At Dress Parade, I shake the General Lee Reenactor's hand. Supper is free Bojangles chicken.

This is September 18th of 2011, and last night I witnessed some cannon firing. I have no watch on but I head up the hill in the early dawn and find most of the 60th Va. and Doug Camper are already here. I help unload biscuits and coffee from S.C.V. Commander Red Barbour's pickup. The bright lights from Bojangles shine over my shoulder where yesterday the 2nd Va. Cavalry pulled a wagon through the drive-thru. I help move some tables for the S.C.V. My hat is off to a member, Skip Fletcher who is walking up the hill flanked by Robert Brown and Terry Williams. I now leave for church as the 28th Va. is attacking the 2nd Va. Cavalry who are responding with cannon fire.

Under the big tent, Evangelist Alan Farley is conducting the service. Colonel Gallion leads in the singing. Commander Barbour and I share the same bale of hay. Terry and Robert sit on the pew, I mean bale of hay, on my other side. After church, a game of 'Redneck Polo' starts; this consists of horsemen with sticks hitting a soccer ball. Allen Jackson had to leave last night so that moves Terry Williams up to 1st Sergeant and morning reports are over an hour late. When Lt. Harrell turns in the report, Skip writes it down on a piece of bark. At this first-time event, we are heavily photographed. Lynell goes back home. Bremen Harrell leads us into battle. Some of the time, Sam Tucker's and my rifles fire. Finally, I run out of ammo and 'die.' Of course, our side carries the day. This is an excellent event!

This is October 1, 2011, and last evening, Lynell and I registered and set up our tent before she went home. The stars fade away as we sit by the fire after a cool night here at Laurel Hill on the birthplace of Confederate Major General J.E.B. Stuart known for his exploits as a cavalryman. I let Travis White borrow the drum of Eric Bower and now I can hear him practicing on it. We have a Roll Call with our rifles. I volunteer for Guard Duty at 11 A.M., then go buy ammo from Mike Broome over at the camp of the 1st Kentucky. Our company is chosen to be Color Company. Captain Harrell not being here, 1st Sergeant Jackson now leads us. Bobby Harris, carrying a Virginia flag, is our Battalion Flag bearer. I march with fixed bayonet off his right shoulder. At the top of the hill to where we march, a Dress Parade of two hundred Confederates plus Yankees is held. Afterward, the ceremony is held where the huge 2nd National Confederate flag is raised.

My brother David drops in for a visit and look-see around. The Davis Family and Captain Harrell come in. David and I go to the Sutlers, meeting Officers Gallion and Switzer along the way. I am thankful that Officer Gallion thinks we do not look alike. Lynell comes in. After company drill, we go to the sutlers to share a lemonade and a Navajo taco.

The Lone Ivy String Band is playing live as they did on the radio last night. Among those listening now are sisters Carolyn Hanchey and Melanie Walker. Lynell and I meet John and Anna LeViner at registration. They go to the nearby home of Robert and Dianne Stanley to leave their dog, Sophie. I go on guard duty with Travis White.

We eventually fall in and march off to battle. Cannons fire sending forth fire and smoke rings. My son John is 'shot' but I live to avenge his 'death.' We clean rifles. The four of us get supper from the Sutlers. John and his wife, Anna, go on the Candlelight Tour. Lynell and I sleep in the truck giving them the tent to sleep in. David Cooper is back.

This is the next morning and over at the campfire, John and I are enjoying cups of hot noodles until he has to go on guard duty with Terry Williams. They are guarding the same bridge that Travis and I guarded yesterday. John comes straight from duty into formation. The Battalion marches up the hill for a Dress Parade. Travis White beats the drum from Eric Bower as he marches alongside of a Yankee drummer providing music for the parade. Yesterday, it was two Yankee drummers. We have Battalion Drill. Back at camp, John Anna, Lynell, and I go up the hill where Alan Farley of Reenactors Missions for Christ is holding a church service. At the fry bread place, we share some food. Captain Harrell gets a new pair of brogans. Back down the hill, my brother David comes in on his birthday. Jonathan Wilson comes in to lend his experience in the upcoming battle. We hear another sermon at the camp as Allen Jackson preaches in camp. Later on, Bobby, from the 28th, plays the spoons and sings accompanied by 51st members Mike on fiddle and Larry on banjo. John and I take some items to the vehicles. When we return, we prepare for battle.

Today, Ben is on my left and James, with a Bonnie Blue Flag, is on my right. We are the Color Company again today. We wait near some woods; as we wait, Colonel Gallion throws a black walnut as one would a baseball. In the battle, we do some charging today as we take the Yanks. Lynell and Anna have gone home. John and I pack the tent to take with us.

This is the evening of October 14, 2011, and Lynell and I arrive at Middleton, Virginia, at registration for the Battle of Cedar Creek. Corporal Brown and Skip Fletcher help us set up. On the way to get parked, we get stuck in the mud. Lynell prays and says "Angels push us out."

This is October 15, 2011, and during the night, a strong wind with rain came through the area. Before dawn, I take a walk under the full moon. I cook sausage over the campfire so Lynell and I can have breakfast. I hear a black Confederate soldier on the street beside us whistling as he goes to fill his canteen with water. Captain Harrell is not here. The 51st soldiers here are Jackson, Brown, Fletcher, Pendleton, and me. We fall in with the 1st Kentucky who are also the Color Company. At the Dress Parade, General Cornett tells us that we have a new insurance company. Art Wingo disperses information to company representatives. The Longstreet's Corp 'Soldier of the Year' award is given out to three soldiers this year, but no accomplishments are said of any. Lynell and I go to the Sutlers and get 3 bee's wax candles, cleaning patches, and a new nipple for my rifle. On our way back to camp, we meet Skip Fletcher who tells us of an informative CD at a Sons of Confederate Veterans table. I go back to Sutler Row and get 2 free CDs. They are entitled 'The Truth Concerning the Confederate Battle Flag' by Pastor John Weaver. Captain Harrell, Mrs. Anita, George, and Esther Davis come in to join us.

We go to battle as a company. Esther gets wet black powder put on her face as this is a tradition with soldiers who are entering their first battle. This is a warning so others will know to look out for and help them. We 'Charge Bayonets' to drive the Yankees. Once after we have fired, General Shelton brushes by me on his way to the front. I soon take a 'hit.' The previously silent cannons now open up, firing over me. The battle rages on to end over by the 'Heater House'. Back in camp, we clean rifles. 1st Sgt. Jackson asks me to keep an eye on the fire. We cook supper over the fire and sit around it as we chat with Skip and Beverly.

This is October 16, 2011, and we slept snugly in our cots here on the 1864 Cedar Creek Battlefield. A morning trip to the 'sinks' reveals an awakening camp plus the last sounds off in the distance of the dawn tactical. Mike Pendleton flanked by Cpl. Brown and myself, posts Company Colors. Skip Fletcher takes pictures. I put two pans of food on the fire grate for Lynell to cook. Captain Harrell is not here and so we fall in with the 1st Kentucky for Dress Parade. General Cornett presents the Charles E. Hylton Longstreet's Corp Scholarship Award to Patrick Smith, a three-year V.M.I. Cadet, then reads an informative Thank You message. Back at camp, George and Esther Davis have completed their long walk back from the parking lot where they stayed last night. Several of us go to the camp of the 1st Kentucky, and then march off to a spot where a Canadian film crew takes some footage of us advancing. An actor wears a wig and makeup. We clean rifles.

Captain Harrell and Mrs. Anita show up with new hats! Seven soldiers including officers comprise the 51st Virginia today. The 1st Kentucky is Color Company and carries our Battle Flag into battle. The camera crew comes with us. We give the 'Rebel Yell' as Henry Kidd is one of the officers out front leading us. Over my left shoulder, I can see the 'Heater House,' then we have to fall back. I run out of ammo.

The black man whose tent is behind mine is a U.S. Marine doing a C.S. Marine impression. When I joined the S.C.V. in 1992, the uniform I had made was a C.S. Marine one. I give him a bumper sticker that says, 'Remember Honor the South's Black Confederate Soldiers'. I still have one on my truck.

This is November 4, 2011, and Lynell and I have arrived here at Ft. Branch on the Roanoke River just passed Hamilton, North Carolina. We register, then find General Shelton of the 1st Kentucky easily. The captain of the 28th Va. and Bobby Compton are here.

This is the morning of November 5, 2011, and we slept good in our tent under a tall Carolina pine. We are tied in with the 1st Kentucky and they post Colors. They have cooked a big breakfast over the fire and Jay insists on us joining in. I buy some ammo from Bobby Compton whose tent is across the Company Street. I take some pictures of the fort and surrounding areas. Lynell had breakfast in the cot and has hardly left the tent on this cool, cloudy, windy morning. I go to the now open museum. I pass by where folks will be cooking the evening meal of deer, pig, and vegetables. At the Sutlers, I hear a man telling of his son's war injuries. He is in the U.S.M.C. and is going back overseas. I see Daniel Young, the blacksmith, and we discuss the recent grave marker dedication. I talk to a Sutler who helped start the S.C.V. camp in Whiteville, NC and knows Layton Dowless. Layton and I both have Samuel Dowless in our ancestry. I get a 'Great Seal of the Confederacy' patch and a cork.

First Call is at 10:30 AM for a tactical, then a battle for spectators. A Yankee and I help two older gentlemen roll a cannon out in front of the museum for display. Three Soldiers representing the 28th and I, representing the 51st, fall in with the few soldiers from the 1st Kentucky to form a company. We march into cotton fields and woods. We spot some Yankees across a pond from us. We take a break and I eat some jerky. We meet up with more Confederates and fire on advancing Yanks.

I clean my rifle at camp then take the Battle Flag of the 51st to the fort for pictures. We are served a big free meal. We get to see cannon firing at night. During the night, the time changes and we gain an hour. About 4 AM, we get up to pack what we didn't last evening. Jay bids us a safe journey. We are at Nags Head, North Carolina, when the sun rises over the Atlantic Ocean. We are taking the long way home so that we can see my son Michael at Chesapeake, Virginia. It is reminiscent of the time I left Ft. Branch with Michael and his brother John when they were kids and we stopped by the ocean on our way home.

It is now December 3, 2011, and time for the Annual Stuart Christmas Parade. Lynell and I show up in our period attire across from Moody Funeral Home, our assembly point each year. Our parade entry is eighteen people strong, Jud being the last one to come in. We step off about thirteenth in a field of 130 entries. Curtis Spence and I are up front with the 'gators' on as part of our uniform. Between us, we are carrying the banner proclaiming the Wharton-Stuart Sons of Confederate Veterans Camp #1832. Sonny Spence pulls a trailer on which Lynell and others ride. Volleys are fired; there are large crowds. I see my brother David down on Main Street.

This is December 9, 2011, and the Wharton-Stuart S.C.V. Camp is holding its Christmas Banquet at the Reynolds Homestead in Critz, Virginia. Over fifty people are in attendance. We have a big meal and Allen Jackson has a new girlfriend. Captain Harrell's crew come in late.

Chapter 7 – 2012

This is January 14,2012, and, in the dark, Lynell and I dressed in our period attire arrive at M&M's Store off Highway 58 to meet up with others on our way to Lexington, Virginia, for the annual Lee-Jackson Day Commemoration. Shannon Brown, S.C.V. 1st Lt. Commander, and his wife are the only ones to show. We travel to Bassett Forks to meet up with Judson. Gene and Pat Reamey are headed to Lexington also. With Jud in tow, we all listen to the CD "The Truth Concerning the Confederate Battle Flag'. Our entourage makes one stop on our way up. It is very cold and windy as the crowd assembles at the grave of Stonewall Jackson for the beginning of our Lee-Jackson remembrance.

Corporal Brown, his daughter, and his brother are here and will march in the parade with us later. Brandon Dorsey opens up the proceedings. A group sing and play instruments. We all sing "Amazing Grace" and "Dixie". Good greetings come from B. Frank Ernest. There is a wreath laying ceremony, and the Lord's Prayer is prayed. Judson falls in with the Stonewall Brigade Honor Guard of the 5th Va. to join in the firing of a three-volley salute. Taps is played. A plane circles overhead pulling a streamer that reads, "Shame on Lexington, Honor Lee and Jackson." A Confederate flag can be seen on the banner as well. We march down the hill through town. I carry our 51st Company Confederate Battle Flag. Many Confederate flags are here where the town council will not put them up. The parade ends on the V.M.I. parade ground. Lynell goes to the Lee Chapel.

Pictured here are Shannon Brown and his wife at Lee Chapel.

This is February 4, 2012, and the annual meeting of the 51st Va. Inf. Co. D is held at our house here at Buffalo Ridge, about three miles from the original muster grounds of Company C which was soon changed to Company D. Past midnight, I continue to put pictures on four poster boards and write captions. About 2 AM, I build fires in the den fireplace heater insert and basement wood stove. I go to bed about 2:30 AM to get up to start work after 6 AM. I am beating out a door mat when Judson drives up in his freshy painted Blazer. Lynell is busy as a bee in the kitchen. The chicken she is frying up will later get quickly gone.

We move furniture in the den. Judson and I go to borrow three tables and some metal folding chairs from our church. At the house, we set them up and he goes for more chairs. The wind begins to blow hard. Jud and I bring back ice from the store just up from the old muster grounds, Country Convenience Market. Allen Jackson is the first to arrive. About three minutes to twelve, Beverly drives up with Skip. He is recovering from an accident in which, by no fault of his, his hand was injured in a wood splitter. Judson is the man of the hour, out parking cars in the rain. We have a good crowd of at least 24 people and soon begin eating. I love the chicken and dumplings Mrs. Anita brings. Most eat downstairs in the den. I play "the 1996 Gettysburg at Fairfield" video.

Seven events are brought before the floor. Election of Captain goes to Lester Harrell, position of Lieutenant goes to Mike Pendleton, and that of 1st Sergeant to Bremen Harrell. The whole meeting is four hours. I help Jud take back the tables and chairs.

This is March 9, 2012, and the time for the 51st Va. Infantry's Annual Camp of Instruction. I head out for South Boston, Virginia, making stops for provisions on the way. I see Allen Jackson who gave me directions to this site in the country. I get put up in a log cabin at last. I start a fire in the woodstove and see a mouse run along one of the interior logs.

This is the morning of March 10, 2012, and during the night, I got up from my cot under the window and put wood in the stove. In this cabin by the lake, 1st Sgt. Harrell also has a cot. His dad, our Captain, is on the bottom bunk with 2nd Sgt. Jackson on the top bunk. Above Jackson in the loft is Private Sam Davis.

In another cabin a way off is George and Roger. They come down after daylight. The Harrells cook bacon and eggs on the stove.

Private Terry Williams, Corporal Robert Brown, and Lieutenant Mike Pendleton all come in camp to join us. 1st Sgt. Harrell, Private Sam Davis, and I post Colors on a peninsula in the nearby lake which could pass for a pond. Members of the 18th Va. with their 1st Sgt Kyle join us for drill. I see the other two ponds on this beautiful property owned by Kyle's family.

Up drives a man with three soldiers to give us all a look at Revolutionary War British and German uniforms and I think a War of 1812 impression.

He has ten sets of uniforms and ten firelock muskets and is seeking recruits. Next weekend, they will be at Guilford Courthouse. The Captain, Mike, and some of the others fire the musket that uses the flint.

We break for lunch. I pay Mike ten dollars for Buchanan registration. The 18th comes down and then we all march out for more drill near one of the ponds. After a while, we break up into companies. We go up near another pond while they roll some rounds. I am sent on a scout. Out across a broom-straw field, we skirmish and fight with the 18th a bit. At least two new guys are on hand. We get back to the cabin. All of the 51st privates leave but me. Kyle and a friend stay at the cabin to talk with us a while.

This is March 11, 2012, and we spend a restful night in this cabin at South Boston under a nearly full moon. I get up several times in the night to put wood on the fire. Lieutenant Pendleton stays in his vehicle. He, 2nd Sgt. Jackson, and I retire the company Colors which have been up all night. Heavy frost is on the windshield of the truck. Kyle and Pat come down to clean and we all spend a lot of time talking and telling war stories.

This is March 17, 2012, and the only Rev. War event I will be in. I decided to try my hand at it and avail myself of the opportunity. As I had told Judson, who was not at the Camp of Instruction, he wishes to try this also. I have always been interested in history and my family history. I had heard a high-ranking officer was in our Revolutionary background. Since at this time I didn't know of any American ones, I thought we may have one on the British side. Jud and I meet up to carpool down to present day Greensboro, North Carolina. At the Guilford Courthouse battleground, we spot Allen Jackson about 10 A.M. The man with the uniforms is not here yet. He comes in while we are at the Sutlers. We are set up near a pond; he issues us clothing and equipment which includes muskets. We change clothes and go into training.

There are eleven of us who represent British Marines today. We are told to load and fire over the lake or pond if you will. Two muskets do not go off, Judson's and mine. A guy named Patrick gets them to go off. Our weapons are then checked before we march off in step. We have a break in the woods before the battle begins. Jud and I are going into our first Revolutionary reenactment without having fired the flintlock or firelock as I hear it called. I get off one shot in the woods where we face some frontiersmen-looking Militia. We advance into a field and I get off a few shots at what must be the Continental Army. I had to wipe off the flint to keep the gun firing. At the end, we fix bayonets, charge, and stick ground by the fallen Americans. As we march off, sweat drips from my tri-cornered hat. Jud and I are on the gun cleaning crew.

This is April 27, 2012, and Lynell and I register at Buchanan, Virginia. Cpl. Brown helps us set up the tent. Some of us buy black powder. I start up the company campfire. The captain arrives. A couple of trains rumble across the James River from us during the night as we lay snug as bugs in our tent eight paces from the pickup.

Just before daylight, birds compete with Interstate 81 traffic as to who will be the loudest. I heat sausage over the company fire and serve Lynell breakfast in her cot. I get to carry our flag, being flanked by Private Sam Tucker of the 18th Va. and Cpl. Brown, with acting 1st Sgt. Jackson calling commands as Colors are posted. I fix up a dozen rounds from powder I got last night. Six of us drill as Capt. Harrell, Lt. Pendleton, and Sgt. Jackson go to another Officer's Meeting. The Davis family come in to set up as Terry Williams had done earlier. In the tent, I fix up more cartridges as Lynell makes a sandwich. Outside now, there is lightning, thunder, and rain. Across the street I go to join others of the company at Faith Community Fellowship Church, located beside the Copper Top Café. I get coffee and some bake sale goods. I can only share the sweets with Lynell back at the tent seeing how she does not drink coffee. We walk to a corner of town for more food and some ice.

At camp, the soldiers form up and a Weapons Inspection is conducted in the rain. We march up to engage some Yankees on a street adjacent to a bank I fought around last year. Up on Main Street, there is more fighting, a lot of ammo is wasted and I have only three caps left when the firing stops. I will ready more rounds before we march out to await the second battle. I take pictures of cannon fire. We are Color Company today. I am soon 'killed.'

At camp, we clean rifles and buy beeswax candles from a salesman. Over in Town Park, a free meal is served to reenactors. Company members walk and pose on the footbridge over the James as I take pictures. Today, we were visited by Jeff and son Eric Bower!

This is April 29, 2012, and a train and a rain came through last night. We awake here in our tent in Buchanan by the river to an overcast morn. In a frying pan, I cook our breakfast we eat in the tent. Chaplain Jackson conducts Church Call which is held while we are seated around the fire. Skip and Beverly Fletcher come in before the battle as they did yesterday. Skip has a protective glove he wears on his injured hand. George Davis captures a bat that was scaring folks; we will set about to scare Yanks. Mrs. Anita is dressed as an Artillery soldier today, as she is to be a 'powder monkey' on Chuck Carter's cannon crew. It is a sight to see her kissing the captain before and after the battle. When she is on the crew, 1st Sgt. Jackson has us render a Present Arms. We are Color Company again. Sam Davis our flagbearer goes down, and Sam Tucker carries the flag throughout the rest of the battle. As we close in, one of their cannon blasts 'decimates' the 28th Va. on our left. Our Captain, who is also our Battalion Commander, is down by this time. We 'decimate' their cannon crew and take the cannon. Only five Yankees are left to surrender. Red Barbour is the announcer and we fight in Town Park.

This is May 26, 2012, and once again I am in a Confederate uniform and with my best girl. We ride to Rocky Mount, Virginia. On the way, we see dozens of German Baptists also known as Dunkards. I hear thousands are coming for a gathering of some type in the County. We park below the Courthouse and see Terry and Joan Williams, Robert Brown, his wife, and son who are here already. Some 60th Virginia members and Doug Camper come in. Members of the Fincastle Rifles S.C.V. #1326 are here. Judson and Melody arrive but she has to leave. George and Sam Davis, Lester and Anita Harrell join us.

Skip Fletcher hands out white gloves for us to wear. The street is blocked off and Commander Harrell marches us up in front of the old Courthouse. Present Arms and speeches are given. Wreathes are laid, one by our Capt. Harrell. Jud's friend, Andy Doss, is here in a Revolutionary War uniform with others as well.

An Air Force ROTC represents too at this Memorial Service. Jud sees Virgil Goode, Presidential Candidate, here. Jud now rides in back of my truck and we follow Skip to his house. Some of the 51st are here, Beverly is busy in her kitchen and Skip is at his grill. Much food and fun are had by all, Allen Jackson especially as he falls out of the hammock in the yard.

. After Lynell and I get home, we have Terry, Joan, Robert, his wife, and their son Kevin stop in to pick some cherries.

This is Saturday June 2, 2012, and the first part of the day we spent on a trip to Christiansburg, Va., to see grandson Oron who has just learned to walk and talk. We get back and I get ready and go to the site of the Battle of Martinsville, Va. Reenactment located at the Sports Complex beside the Smith River. At Registration, I didn't have to sign anything or pay anything. I get in with a company that I don't even know the name of. The soldier beside me is from Ellerbe, North Carolina. I see a puff of smoke then hear the first shot of the battle. The Cavalry go at it. One man is thrown from his horse twice. The Bryants are in the Artillery. We deploy as skirmishers, and after advancing and firing awhile I take a 'hit.' While laying wounded, I learn from the captain that this is the 30th North Carolina. After the battle, I buy black powder, caps, cartridge tubes, and a cork.

This is June 8, 2012, and the start of another of the 150th Anniversary Events. It is Cross Keys and Port Republic being held on the Cedar Creek battlefield, so it is at least still in Virginia. Just off Interstate 81, I drive past Registration as it has been moved from the usual registration spot. I show a man slips of paper we got in the mail as we were preregistered, and he gives each of us a medallion of 'Stonewall' Jackson on a ribbon to hang about our necks. In Middleton, we turn to go to the backside of the Cedar Creek battlefield. We see our company sign on the back of our Captain's tent then we see Mike Pendleton who says the sign being there was Skip Fletcher's idea. Thank You, Skip! Chuck Carter helps Lynell and me set up the tent. At 10 P.M., I am driving to park the pickup about a mile away across the road. About fifteen Sutlers are set up, but most are closed so I go in two.

This is the early morning of June 9, 2012, and we awake to receive a few tweets, bird tweets that is. We venture out to visit the 'sinks' under a real half-moon. Out by the company fire, I heat up a full frying pan of sausage patties and am glad to share with Officers Brown and Jackson. I learn Allen Jackson is the Adjutant to Colonel Bill Russell who is 2nd Brigade Commander; Barry Woods is 1st Brigade Commander, Officer Terry Shelton is Longstreet Corps Commander, and General Dave Cornett is the Overall Confederate Commander. Our Company Colors are posted close to our tent. Sergeant Terry Williams commands the Color Detail of Fletcher, Brown, and a man from the 5th Virginia.

I get in a nap before time to accouter up for Dress Parade. A Brigade comes up the hill with a black Confederate soldier in their ranks. The 130 men here from Longstreet Corps assemble. A man who has joined us for this weekend stands beside me. His name is Melvin Lester. General Cornett addresses the troops. We do some drill before returning to camp. I buy a three-dollar bag of ice that goes in the cooler. Colonel Bill Russell stops by in camp, I buy from him a 150th Anniversary battle of Fredericksburg medallion for 10 dollars, I give him a photo from the 145th Gettysburg event.

I have bologna and cheese sandwiches, strawberries, and almonds. We go out to the Corps' assemble point where our rifles are Inspected. We march out in a field of tall grass to a point above the Heater House and below highway. Distance shots are heard but still no Yanks seen. We advance and it is our lot to be in the creek bed. Over rocks, holes, dips, and rough terrain we go now 'pushing' Yanks, but we do not fire yet. Colonel Russell goes down briefly when one leg goes to about the knee in a large hole. The fight is short and sharp. On our right, Barry Woods is bringing on the 1st Brigade, and on our left more of our boys in gray are carrying the day, also. I can only get off a few well aimed shots. On my last time loading, my rifle butt is muddied; as I bend down to wipe my hand off in the grass, Colonel Russell comes by putting his hand on my back, possibly favoring an injured leg.

Now at camp, it is time to clean my rifle. I find some chicken salad and strawberries. Most of us find some shade over under the captain's tent fly. A Color Detail of Williams, Brown, Lester, and Bandy retire the Colors. Over on a hill, a water truck showers a few folks in an attempt to cool them down. As night comes on, Mike Pendleton cranks up the fiddle and a few 'flat foot'.

Chuck and Carol occupy the tent next to ours. Conversation continues into the night out on the company street.

This is June 10, 2012, and we slept well here on the Cedar Creek battlefield last night. I share the grate with others as I cook breakfast over the fire, then serve Lynell breakfast. Company Colors are posted by Williams, Brown, Fletcher, and Carter. I make up rounds as I did last evening and fill up the cartridge box. Soon, we go out to Dress Parade. A Corps photo is taken. The front row plus the Officers will kneel. Music for the Parade today consists of two fifes and a drum. There is a brief Battalion Drill afterwards. Soon Allen Jackson has Church Call at Captain Harrell's tent fly. He will deliver a good sermon. In attendance in the packed crowd

is Colonel Bill Russell. I get lunch, it must be 90 degrees. A 'new' couple is being welcomed and having 'the ropes' explained to them. We get ready and go out to have Weapons' Inspection. We march off in the tall grass to wait in the hot sun. It is a great photo opportunity as the 'Stonewall'

Jackson reenactor, as well as General Cornett and Staff are riding about. Spectators are high on a hill above the Heater House.

We now push and shoot at the small bands of Yankees we see. At one point, the two battle lines collide, and the Yanks lose again.

Capt. Harrell has us drift back in the direction of the parking lot. The way the battle was planned to be going in before the battle. A Virginia State Trooper stops traffic to let us out. I drive back to camp to load up. It is so dry that the ground clothes are not wet.

This is Saturday the 16th of June 2012, and day of this year's Covered Bridge Festival here in Patrick County, Virginia. My oldest son John and I are in Confederate attire when we arrive on site at Jack's Creek Covered Bridge hardly five miles or less from my house. We are greeted by Gene Fain. Shannon Brown drives up as does Mike Corns. My tent and the Company tent fly are set up.

Confederate flags, the Bonnie Blue, and Virginia flags are here on display. Sammy Hughes and Terry Williams are here briefly. John, Mike, and myself man the 'booth' awhile. Once, I have a couple of thirteen-year-old boys who seem to be interested in the Sons of Confederate Veterans. I give them some educational literature to read titled "The War for Southern Independence or Slavery? Read the Truthful Statements from our History." John and I go on lunch break after Kenneth Holt and his wife come in to help.

We find something to eat at the food vendors then walk up the road to visit Jack Myers, a fellow truck driver who is now ill. Back at our set up, Crystal Harris, our Smith River Supervisor, comes by to talk. The Duck Race is next. We pack up and the S.C.V. items will be returned to Sammy.

This is September 7, 2012, and time for another 150th Anniversary Event! This one is the battle of Sharpsburg, Maryland. Lynell and I are viewing scenes of the original battlefield much like Judson and I had years before. Although Jud and I had found 'Burnside Bridge', now we get lost trying to find it. We will visit the 'Bloody Lane,' and the 'Sunken Road'. At Boonsbourgh, Maryland, we go to Registration, but Lynell has to go to Civilian Registration. We fill out the information requested. We get no schedule, map, pass of any type, or medallion for this big event. We park in a giant field as other vehicles flood in.

I walk up a hard surface road in search of our camp. It is nearly all the way in back of the Confederate camp in a boxed in area. As it is now dark, the only way I am able find our camp is that I hear Skip Fletcher talking. He, his wife Beverly, and Melissa Pendleton are by the fire over by the tent fly. A few tents over by the 28th Va., we find Robert Brown, Terry and Joan Williams. I enjoy talking to Lawhorn of our 28th days. Fifteen years ago, we were at the 135th Sharpsburg event. I walk, carrying no light, looking for the Sutlers and end up in the Yankee camp. I walked through a Yankee Officers' Meeting, twice. Part of the Yankee camp butts up against the Sutlers, I should have known. There I find a Confederate Officers' Meeting going on. I spot our Officers there, Mike Pendleton and Allen Jackson. After the meeting, I learn I need to be in camp at 7 A.M. I buy some German-made caps for $12.95, before going back to check out the sleeping arrangements.

This is September 8, 2012, and we start getting ready for the day before 5 A.M. I eat and we start out walking to camp and, several rest-stops later, arrive by the dawn's early light. Lynell eats breakfast in camp. Today our 51st Va. Infantry Company D consists of eight people: 1st Lt. Mike Pendleton, 1st Sgt. Allen Jackson, 2nd Sgt. Robert Brown, and Privates Travis White, Isaac White, Terry Williams, Skip Fletcher, and me. We all march out to the Dress Parade wearing our green battle shirts with the white trim.

The 1st Kentucky wears their battle shirts, also. We are the smallest company. There are many soldiers in butternut as I would like to be but the rules said otherwise. General Cornett presides over Longstreet Corps. He also leads us in Battalion Drill.

Later comes Company Drill, at one point, I stack seven rifles. Back in camp, Travis cooks bacon over a small fire.

Lynell and I eat from the basket carried in earlier. I talk with General Cornett under his tent fly and show him 8x10's from the Sharpsburg event 15 years ago when he was my Captain. He wants me to tell my brother Judson "hello" and I say, "I will." First Call comes and the 51st is exiting the 'box canyon' in single file between the tents. Our rifles are inspected by Officer Terry Shelton and at the staging area, I stack our rifles once again. I take some pictures before we move out. We are halted on a wooded lane when the wind comes up, thunder rolls, and rain hits. We all turn our backs to it; behind me sits the General on his horse. The spectators at the battlefield scatter. The rain eases up and we move to the edge of the battlefield. As we had loaded before the rain, now my gun finally goes off after the fifth cap is fired. Cannon fire starts on our right. The spectators come back. We wheel to face the Yanks, none of the maneuvers we practiced are used here. I fire a few rounds where I simulate being kicked by my rifle. I take a 'hit' and don't know until after the battle that Travis White took one about twenty yards back. We don't know until after the long battle that soon after our misfortune, the 51st and Longstreet Corps are taken out of the battle. I fall in a good spot. Earlier, 2nd Sgt. Brown and I squeezed water from our sleeves so the ground does not bother me.

Allen Jackson looks forward to the chance to 'whip up on some Yanks' before the first battle. The General surveys troops before battle.

On both sides of me are hundreds if not thousands of troops. There is plenty of firing over my head. Once the Yanks advance by me.

I get close up pictures of Confederates, also. After the battle, we see Melissa and Joan who are among the spectators. At camp, we clean rifles. More rain comes in and the afternoon battle is called off. Travis helps me cross a barb wire fence to get out the back way to the road. Soon, a golf cart gives me a ride to the parking lot. I have my rifle, accouterments, a wooden folding chair, and a blanket covered cooler. Lynell is resting in back of the pickup. We drive out in town to eat then return to a different parking spot.

This is the morning of September the 9th, 2012, and before 4 A.M., here in Maryland, I start my day. Lynell slaps on an 'Icy Hot' on my aching back. I have my rifle and accoutrements as I start out for camp under the light of a half moon. Sounds of loud snoring from some of the tents penetrate into every part of the still camps. At the camp of the 51st Virginia, I sit under the fly in front of 1st Sgt. Jackson's tent. At a fire out front lay two men sleeping. Now all is quiet, then the bugles sound, and folks stir about slowly. I hear Officer Lawhorn of the 28th Va. behind Jackson's tent say he has lost a button. I lost one yesterday. I recall that how fifteen years ago at this event, he was my 1st Sergeant. None of the 51st will be wearing battle shirts today. Isaac White borrows a coat; it even has stripes on it. I have on a grey frock coat with black piping, black wool trousers, and the same black slouch hat of fifteen years ago.

By the light offered from the moon, we march on a soaked path out of camp between the backs of tents barely two feet apart. Skip Fletcher gets out in front of our little formation with some important news. He states that if you are wet like yesterday, don't ever use Medicated Menthol Gold Bond Powder on jock itch because you will always live to regret it. Well, we all set in on how old and aching we are, except Isaac who will be our designated runner. It looks like we will be needing the Life Alert devices when we fall and say 'I cannot get up'. Travis White thinks we need our haversacks filled with supplies such as Gold

Bond, Ben Gay, Ensure, and so on. In reality, the laughing we do is the best medicine we can have. We wait for the 'hardcore' reenactors to emerge. An Officer uses a loud bad word many times as the hundreds of butternut-clad troops come out in the moonlight to assemble in a field.

As the dawn is breaking, we all move to an adjacent field. Here are rail fences and beyond lies a cornfield. Some fellows slept by the fences last night and camp fires still smolder. We cross a fence and stop at the edge of the cornfield. Our Skirmishers soon find Yanks in there. We have to lie down awhile. We now go into the cornfield and fire on the Yankees. Next, a call back to a fence where our Artillery opens up firing through and over us into the cornfield. Concussion shock waves hit us as we hunker down. I look over my right shoulder to see Lt. Mike Pendleton get engulfed in smoke from cannon number 4 that just fired. There are hundreds of troops about. Out of the cornfield soldiers come helping 'wounded' comrades out crying 'open up' as they pass to the rear. On my left come hundreds of Confederate troops that demolish the rail fencing in their path as they rush into the fastly disappearing cornfield. Smoke is the order of the day now. Down the line Henry Kidd is gleefully snaping pictures of soldiers in the smoke. I regret not having my camera as I had this stupid thought that I could not top the good pictures I took yesterday. Once I see Lawhorn about 30 yards away disappear in the smoke searching for the 28th Virginia. The sun now up over our shoulders is an orange ball. Yankees emerge from the smoke and we fall back to the field we came from.

Now everyone takes a long break. People take off accoutrements, lounge about, and eat. Terry, Robert, and I take a walk after we have naps. The 51st ceases to be a company now as Travis and Isaac head on back toward home. The Reverend Allen Jackson holds a Church Service in a shady part of this field before we move on to wait in a staging area. The Fife and Drum Corps keep up our spirits as we endure a long wait. The General and his staff on horseback enjoy the music also. We march over a hill to see lines of the Federals below. Before we can fire a shot, there is a medical emergency. The fighting is stopped so the E.M.S. vehicle can come out on the field. Finally, we get our chance to fire. I pull down to 'fire' on their flagbearer a few times. I start to fall back with a 'wound' in the direction of the parking lot as Confederates are 'driving' the Yanks. I change clothes before Lynell and I exit.

This is September 14, 2012, and after a day's work I arrive here at the Reynold's Homestead in Critz, Virginia, for the 51st Virginia Infantry Company D's Camp for Kids. Sammy Hughes and Chris Washburn are already here. I help set up tents before the kids arrive. In the Learning Center, I read to the boys about the events of last weekend at Sharpsburg and Sammy talks about the Confederate flags.

This is the morning of September 15, 2012, and I spent the night near the old barn in the back of my pickup. Early this morning, we march back down to the nearby Center for breakfast. Lisa Martin, Program Director for the Reynold's Homestead, is here before she is to take her daughter to the Raleigh, N.C. airport to fly to England. The boys are marched back to camp where enlistment papers are filled out, and rifles are issued. I get the boys to drilling. A lad wearing a cast on his arm is our flagbearer. I let each boy shoot my musket. Some parents visit and Chris Washburn arrives on site. We go downstairs of the Learning Center where Chris gives a very informative presentation covering topics such as: Honest Abe wasn't Honest, the North got rich selling slaves, blacks fought for the South, and the Emancipation Proclamation didn't free a single slave. We all have lunch

before leaving back to camp. More drilling before we march out to the slave cemetery. We look around and have our picture taken.

Next, we go to the Rock Spring where they all enjoy wading in the creek. Mr. Foley comes in to help out as his wife had helped last night. The kids play the ageless game of 'hide and seek'. Mike Pendleton comes in to provide banjo music. Captain Sammy Hughes fixes up cane fishing poles and we go down to the ponds. I take more pictures then go to get them developed. On my return, we have supper in the building. I post guards for the evening.

Today is September 16, 2012, and I slept here under the camper shell. Two hard rains fell during the night. The pickup is parked a few yards across a dirt road by an old barn back of the big house. A picture of this barn with its porch across the front is on the front page of this week's local newspaper. Inside the Learning Center hangs the oil painting of it by Lee Farley which won the 'Best in Show' award in the J.E.B. Stuart Art Show. We get up and I march the boys and Sammy's 7-year-old daughter, Hannah, to breakfast. Parent Kenny Foley stays the night to help out. Sammy and I get the kids folders ready. I give Lisa Martin a copy of the 54 quotes entitled 'The War for Southern Independence, or Slavery? Read the Truthful Statements from our History', plus an insert from a Point Lookout Prisoner of War newsletter how a black man started the institution of slavery in Virginia. Copies of these also went in the kids' folders. Sammy among other things had a flag for each kid. The skies are overcast, and it could rain at any minute. It is decided the Graduation Ceremony will be held indoors.

This is September 21, 2012, and we arrive here at Lake Watch Plantation for the Franklin County Civil War Days event. Red Barbour let us park in the handicap area near the facilities. We sleep under the pickup camper shell. Before dawn, we drive to the main parking. I carry my rifle, accoutrements, and a chair to camp. Terry Williams carries a stool for me. Allen Jackson slept in Captain Harrell's tent last night; the captain is expected in today. I get Lynell and me free Bojangles breakfast biscuits. At camp, Jackson, Williams, Brown, and I post

Colors. Later Mike Pendleton comes in to be our Officer at Dress Parade where we are addressed by General Lee. Mike and Melissa Pendleton are in photo on previous page.

Skip Fletcher is this event's Quartermaster. Terry Shelton is this event's Confederate Commander. At one point, I go over to the camp of the 28th Va. and give Sobataka a 1996 Gettysburg at Fairfield D.V.D. I show them 8x10s of the 28th at the 135th Sharpsburg and the photo taken in 2000 of the 28th at V.M.I. Mrs. Anita, Capt. Harrell, 1st Sgt. Bremen Harrell, George Davis, Bethany Davis, Miss. Lill, Sam Davis, Hannah Davis, Ben Davis, and Amber Davis come into camp. Larry Mabe is now here, too. Members of the 18th Va. join us including Sam Tucker still in high school. We do Skirmish Drill before the battle. Cannon fire starts then we are skirmishing up and back. Yankees are behind brush breastworks. The 28th Va. go in the woods to flank them. We charge and the twenty soldiers in the Yank Infantry and a cannon crew are 'decimated'. These Civil War Days have, for Lynell and I, turned into a Civil War Day, just one. Around 7 P.M., a grandson named Declan Leviner is born and tomorrow we must go see him!

This is October 6, 2012, the one day of the J.E.B. Stuart event we have chosen to participate in.

Here at our house, Lynell fixes biscuits to go with the ham she cooked last night. Cooking always precedes a homecoming and that is where we are going tomorrow, but today we drive over still in the county to the J.E.B. Stuart Birthplace in Ararat, Virginia. It is the 22nd Annual Encampment and reenactment. We get registered and get our ribbons before parking beside the vehicles of Jud and Jackson. I walk in camp in time to march up Laurel Hill for the morning Dress Parade; we were told not to take canteens.

After Parade we do Company and Battalion Drill. It is a hot sunny morning. We march under the direction of overall Confederate Commander Terry Shelton to the giant flagpole. Terry Williams, Allen Jackson, and 1st Sgt Bremen Harrell are on the Color Detail. We Present Arms as the large 2nd National Confederate flag is raised. Other 51st members are spotted at the Sutlers. I see Lynell and we get lunch at the frybread place. Bailey Clark is looking for Sammy Hughes. At camp, we hear fiddle and banjo music from Mike Pendleton and Larry Mabe. The ladies of the 51st Va. conduct a Ladies Tea with 1st Ky. Ladies invited to join in under Capt. Lester Harrell's tent fly.

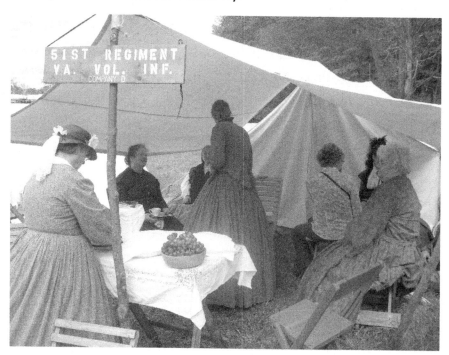

The men march off to await battle. In our company, there are seventeen including Officers. We enter the fight after the skirmishers withdraw. I shoot up a lot of ammo. We have the best volleys on the field. Jud at J.E.B. Stuart is the title of the next photo.

I am wounded in an attempt to conserve ammo for a guy who goes by the name of 'Paycheck' tomorrow. The Surgeon helps me back away then another 'Doctor' puts a rag around my head complete with a 'blood' spot already on it. After battle Officer Shelton saves someone from an 'execution.'

This is December 1, 2012, and time for this year's Stuart Christmas Parade. I sew a button on my black wool trousers; there were no zippers back in the day. Lynell leaves our car at the end of the parade route and, in the pickup truck, we go to where we are staging. There will be ten of us in all in our entry including two soldiers from N.C. (one being Jerry Hobbs), the women, and Sammy's little girl. We are the 14th entry from the front.

My last year's partner carrying the banner, Curtis Spence, is on the banner this year with his Uncle Raymond Spence who I let wear my 'gators.' They are up front of our procession letting folks know we are the Wharton-Stuart Sons of Confederate Veterans camp #1832 from Stuart, Virginia. Next marching is Judson and myself flanking Kenneth Holt who is carrying the Virginia State flag. Sonny Spence comes on driving a big pickup pulling the trailer/float. Mike Corns is on board, also. Lynell throws candy. At the old Courthouse Jud and I fire one double loaded volley, then hear applause.

This is December 7, 2012, and Lynell and I arrive for the 150th Anniversary battle of Fredericksburg, Virginia. We walk in the Comfort Inn and are greeted by Captain Harrell in the lobby. Shortly, Robert Brown walks in from the hallway across from the desk to greet us. Mrs. Anita is here as well as Robert's son Kevin Brown. I hear of others like Skip, Allen, and Bremen are around. I park beside of Skip's big pickup. Lynell and I are in room 103.

This is December 8, 2012, and a phone call from the front desk awakens us here in the Comfort Inn in Spotsylvania, Va. I take a shower and put on my Confederate uniform. Out in the lobby, Union and

Confederate troops are getting breakfast. The grits I spill on my shell jacket only serves to help the impression. I take accoutrements from my room and my rifle from our car; they are put in with others in the back of Skips Dodge truck. He covers them with a slide tarp. Skip drives Chuck, Robert, Terry, and me into an area that looks like a fairground site. Robert and I go to a hanger type building to confirm our registration and pick up our event medallions. Skip parks and we catch a bus ride to a large Confederate camp area. On the bus, I sit next to a reenactor with 20 years of experience; I have only 19 years of reenacting experience. He is looking to hook up with the 18th Va. Now off the bus, I see him walking with Henry Kidd toward camp.

Captain Terry Shelton and the 1st Kentucky are here. We are met by our 3rd Battalion Commander who I do not know by name. He said, "We would be by a parking deck hitting the Yanks in their flank when they came by." This never happened for us, as I noticed later some other soldiers got to do that. Here is where we get the first taste of the biggest way, we will spend most of the rest of our time at this event: waiting, with the emphasis on waiting. We do a great deal of it on the porch of an old abandoned house. I forgot my camera at the Inn, but Skip has his. Pictures are taken of us at the porch. Buses come for us; some are from a Christian school. A Sergeant Major totes around a large branch and talks some smack and we are also informed not to have any cameras or farby stuff out due to all kinds of news media in town. Bill Russell is directing soldiers to the buses. We are in the last group and arrive in the Historic District of Fredericksburg. We disembark and form up on a street facing a house where people with dogs come out. A picture of Lincoln is produced from somewhere and laughter breaks out as comments fly. We march down the street where I get my first view of the Rappahannock River before turning left on a road running parallel to the river. We are marched at the Route Step to a spot on the road beside a parking deck and halted. This is the site of some major waiting today.

The 44th Va. is the next company beside of us; they are our 3rd Battalion Color Company. At one point, I look behind me to see the man I tackled at Spotsylvania when he was dressed in blue. Through a gap in houses, I can see the river below across a small plain. I heard later of two Sutlers which I never see or any sign of a pontoon river crossing either. Sometimes, we are at In Place Rest; at one brief period, we Stack Arms. We are a force to be reckoned with: Captain Lester Harrell, 1st Lt. Mike Pendleton, 1st Sgt. Bremen Harrell, 2nd Sgt. Allen Jackson, Corporal Robert Brown, and Privates Skip Fletcher, Terry Williams, Chuck Carter, another Chuck, Leon Craft, and his grandson, and myself. For this day of battle, I wear my period brogans, black trousers, grey shell jacket, and black slouch hat. Many people walk by, one who stops and talks is Gary Walker, author of some Confederate books. Heads are hanging out of the 5-story parking deck and people are on the roof. The fellows say they have found a new woman for Allen Jackson. She is up at Guyandotte, West Virginia; she is about 6 ft. 8 in. tall with new dental work. Chuck Carter says, "She could keep Allen warm in the winter and provide him shade in the summer." Hundreds of spectators now line the sides of the street.

We hear distance cannon and rifle shots. Our lead company is soon exchanging volleys with advancing Bluecoats. Our Companies fire a few shots then the survivors peel off loading as they go to form up again behind the last company in line. Our time comes to face the fire. Our Captain goes down; Leon gets off only one shot, Shifty, i.e., Terry Williams, is 'killed' after firing three shots. Down the street a way and Skip Fletcher is down. He lies in a contorted position while looking up. We have snipers, I see two in a frame house near the river. A company stalls the Bluecoats briefly hitting their flank as they pass the parking deck. The surviving Confederates now turn up a street.

Four of the 51st remain now: Officers Mike Pendleton and Bremen Harrell, Chuck Carter, and me; then I am the only survivor. I get in with the 24th Va. We are ordered to surrender but I won't turn my rifle upside down. They will have to capture me but they never do. It is over for now. Everyone regroups and stories are told. The captain says he was rolled out of the street, Leon says they carried him off, and Skip says he was photographed a lot. Chuck Carter gives me some food from his haversack. We are marching parallel to the river again, this time by some Bluecoats. Mike Pendleton and Allen Jackson start singing some song about 'killing

Yankees.' We turn up a street and march several blocks, seeing plenty of old shops and houses. Once I crane my neck to look up at a tall Church steeple. We are halted, turn in a lane, halted, and Stack Arms. This will be another place to wait.

We are beneath Maye's Heights at the Sunken Road. I rest against a wall. Some go off to the right to explore; I will, too. I see a statue of Sgt. Kirkland from South Carolina, who went into 'no man's land' to give water to the wounded on both sides. He would later be killed in the battle of Chickamauga, Georgia. At part of the wall still here today, a sign that reads 'Do not touch, Stay Off' goes unheeded. A N.P.S. Ranger walks by doing nothing as school kids play on it and reenactors sit on it. Skip lets me use his camera to take a few pictures. I shake hands with Frank Mosley, Captain of the 24th Va. who also works at Barnes & Nobel booksellers at the Christiansburg, Va. store. We Take Arms, march across the road, and continue marching up on a hillside. It appears to be part of Marye's Heights. We are up behind a wall made of 2x4's and plywood. The outside is painted to look just like a rock wall. I see General Cornett for the first time at this event. He calls up Captain Frank Mosley and has him face the troops. He is then honored for his three decades in the Confederate Service.

Troops crowd up next to the wall, lined 4-deep. Now more waiting as the shadows grow long. Finally, the Federals come up driving in our skirmishers before them. Our first two ranks let go a volley. The soldier at the wall is to shoot at least four times then peel off to the rear. Our company has two lines of four men each. Rifles get loaded and passed to the front. Once, I hear Chuck Carter on his turn at the wall saying, "Gimme, Gimme," reaching for another rifle while watching the Yankees pile up. Two cannons fire from above our position. Concussion waves roll over us. We march up beside the cannon as others of our troops file in to have their time at the wall. At one point, I am firing my rifle with my foot against a cannon wheel. Chuck Carter comes and makes some space between us and the cannon which continues to fire. I use my ammo to load whatever rifle is sent to me until it is gone.

This morning my cartridge box was full, and now I only have eleven caps left. As a bugle now sounds ending the fight, the cannon fires one last time. With my hat on the end of my barrel, I hold my rifle high. Taps are played by a lone bugle, and everyone is still and silent for a few more moments as we remember the terrible amount of pain and suffering and bloodshed and dying of 150 years ago. The ground in front of the wall is almost a blue carpet. We can see a reenactor portraying Sergeant Kirkland with a canteen taking water to the wounded. We clear weapons and march across the street to wait for the buses. All the waiting we have had to do today has been worth it. I see General Cornett talking; behind him is the University of Mary Washington sign. At this time, I didn't know it would be the last time I would see him; or to be more accurate, I haven't seen him since.

CHAPTER 8 – 2013

This is Saturday, February 2, 2013, and the day of this year's Annual 51st Va. Inf. Co. D's meeting. Lynell is in the kitchen cooking up some fried chicken. It will soon be loaded with the ham, potato soup, biscuits, rolls, deviled eggs, pickles, banana nut bread, fruit, and chocolate éclair. On our journey to Captain Harrell's house for the meeting, we see Allen, as well as Terry and Robert. Lynell, Bremen, and I carry in the food. Allen comes in and helps Lester, Bremen, his new girlfriend, and me string up fishing line with small clothespins on it. More members arrive. Skip has some pictures he gives out. After we start eating, Chuck and Carol come in from the Appomattox area of the state. The meeting starts and the captain 'steps' out of his office. He will become an Officer on General Shelton's Staff. Allen Jackson gets the most votes to become the new 1st Sgt. and Bremen becomes the 2nd Sergeant. The only one voted on for Captain is Mike Pendleton and he gets it by unanimous decision. Most of the 58 8x10 reenacting photos hanging on the small clothespins go out at the meeting's end. All the money I get for them gets donated to the company. At one point, we have twenty-five people present. Now, we load up to leave.

This is Saturday, April 6, 2013, and a Company Drill has been called for at Terry and Joan Williams place in the country. Allen Jackson calls before he comes to our house to follow Lynell and me to the Williams' place. We pass by Jacks Creek Covered Bridge on the way. Skip and Beverly Fletcher are here when we arrive. Terry shows me around, then Captain Pendleton comes in and the drill begins. We practice Fix Bayonet plus loading and firing positions. The three women go to Lester Harrell's house to attend a baby shower for Amber Davis. We are practicing marching when Lester Harrell with George, Ben, and Sam Davis drive up. We do Fix Bayonet and Load drill. After a break, we do some marching maneuvers and Stack Arms drill. Terry gets some burgers and 'dogs' on the

outside grill. Mrs. Anita, Amber, and Bremen's girlfriend come in. Seth Harrell is here as is Mrs. Melissa, too. A good time is had by all.

This is April 12, 2013, and time for the 150th Anniversary Battle of Williamsburg, Va. which is being held at Endview Plantation. Lynell and I arrive on site and go in at an old house to sign our names. That's it; there are no passes, instructions, or medallions. We were already preregistered anyway. A Sutler Row is nearby, I buy some C.C.I. caps and a bag of paper ladies, the tubes black powder is put in to make a cartridge. I talk with a black college student who is very knowledgeable on true history. I give him copies of the 54 quotes from General Lee and others plus the info how a black man had the law changed so he could own his black endured servant for life, introducing slavery in Virginia. We find the camp and Skip and Beverly Fletcher help us set up. Terry and Joan Williams' tent is close to ours. I park the pickup then feed the fire.

This is April 13, 2013, and we are reenacting the March 29th, 1863, Battle of Williamsburg, Virginia. A strong wind during the night blew a system out to sea. I cook sausage in a frying pan and sit around the fire with Skip and Terry; Chuck is in the cabin he and his wife stayed in last night. For now, we are it for the 51st Virginia.

We all get to camp under the trees at this event. We go over to the camp of the 1st Kentucky to fall in with them. Mr. Broome is with us awhile, even though, he will soon be having surgery. Our Captain, who says that this is his first time being a captain, marches us out to Dress Parade.

As far as I know, this is the first Dress Parade presided over by General Shelton since becoming Commander of Longstreet Corps. I remember being on this field when General Hillsman who started the Corps was in charge. General Shelton has us doing some manual of arms at this parade. His new saying is, 'Forward the Corps!' We break up to do first Company Drill, then Battalion Drill. At camp, I film some with my new small hand held camcorder. I've put black tape over the name, brand, logo, and so forth to remain more inconspicuous when filming. Lynell and I have sandwiches from the tent. Most everyone goes to see what the Sutlers have to sell. Soldiers of the 51st go back over to the camp of the 1st Kentucky. The combined total is nine people. Our 1st sergeant is a 19-year-old lady; a 20-year-old lady private stands on my left. About 2 P.M., the Reenactment of the 150th Anniversary of Wise's March 29, 1863 Attack on Williamsburg begins. Tomorrow, it will be the April 11, 1863 Battle Reenactment. I see Yankee skirmishers but no cavalry. Our cavalry is on the field a good amount of time. I believe they are the 14th, Virginia. Bill Russell Commands the companies we are with.

The Yanks have come out of their fort to fight. We advance a good distance firing as we go. Skip goes down putting on a good show in the process. I am 'wounded' and lay with my back to the spectators. I try to film some action with my camcorder, but I am not having much luck. I soon quit. We march back to clean rifles. Skip and Terry fix the tip of my bayonet scabbard. Carol and Joan go to sell chances on a quilt to raise funds for the company. Beverly buys a book cover for Lynell. I talk to my son Michael on the phone who lives in Chesapeake, Virginia. I carry two buckets of water up so we can have it in case the fire gets out. I walk by the old house with its out-buildings to the Sutlers. I purchase a nipple for my Armisport 3-band Enfield rifle, Ballistol multi-purpose cleaner, and a small glass bottle for Lynell. She is cooking over the fire when I get back. For supper we have Kielbasa, onions, and rice. Lynell pulls another tick off of me. Before dark there is a fire fight, the Yanks attack. I guard the back of the camp; the Yanks are defeated.

This is April 14, 2013, and before 4 A.M., I have pulled off two more ticks. By light, I pull off another one which means the total is now at seven. I cook breakfast over the fire as Skip, Terry and I swap stories. I serve Lynell breakfast in her cot. A little later and I see Terry showing Robert Brown, his wife, and their son Kevin into camp. Robert replaces Chuck as he and his wife left their cabin early today in order to sight-see in the historic areas near us. Soon the four of us go over to the camp of the 1st Kentucky to make nine of us in the company.

On this sunny day, we march out to Dress Parade. Gen. Shelton has us practice a Secure Arms. One drum provides music for the parade. We do Company Drill. At Battalion Drill, we do Wheels also. General Shelton conducts the entire drill while we are at Shoulder Arms, enough said.

Lynell is not feeling well. Church is held under the big tent. Once when I am walking, I salute Gen. Shelton who is riding in a golf cart. At the tent, Lynell and I have sandwiches. Joan Williams makes a public announcement; Terry has been banned from sleeping with her except when it is cold and maybe a few other exceptions. Shifty got a little too shifty during the night and Joan found herself off the mattress.

The four of us soldiers go over once again to the 1st Ky. and then march out for a Weapons Inspection.

The 47th Va. is our Color Company at this event. Beside of General Shelton walks Capt. Steve DiCarlo, his Color bearer. I have seen this man at his post of duty going on twenty years now and he was there before I came along. He rode alongside Corps Commanders Hillsman, Moffit, maybe Shumate who served a short time, and Cornett, carrying the First National Confederate flag, perhaps, the same one he now carries. We stage back in some woods. I film a little. The Skirmishers start causing a ruckus. Spectators line the right for perhaps a couple hundred yards. As yesterday, we start for the fort with the moat. We waste an exorbitant amount of ammunition while the Yanks don't fire much. Our company fires some perfect volleys, which means all of our rifles fire together to make a sound as of one loud gun. The more our men run low on ammo, the more our 'hits' increase. I'm doing the wounded thing so I can sneak and film a little. The 51st suffers 100% causalities again today. We knew if one of us went down, we would already have 25% causalities. Skip and I pour canteen water down our hot barrels to have instant hot water. Skip, the veteran reenactor is in the next picture.

Hot water being a first step in rifle cleaning. I get the pickup and we load up. We are followed out by the Browns. I took a wrong turn, but they didn't. Eventually, we stop on our way to see granddaughter Abby! The tick count topped out at nine.

On April 20, 2013, Confederate Memorial Day is observed here in Stuart, Va. at the old Courthouse. Brother Judson is our Color Sergeant here to command our Honor Guard. Allen Jackson is the guest speaker. We have three rifles from Henry County joining us in our volleys.

This is April 27, 2013, and last evening we arrived at Buchanan, Va. to set up. Lynell and I slept as snug as bugs in a rug last night in our tent on our cots by the James River. I call Attention on the Street before 1st Sgt. Williams, Cpl. Brown, Pvt. Craft, and myself salute our new Captain Pendleton. I stick a frying pan of sausage in the fire and soon we are having breakfast. Several go to a breakfast in town and come back of reports of it not being too well. Lynell and I go to the Sutlers, and I get some tubes for cartridges but find no powder. The Officers go to a meeting. George, Bethany, and Sam Davis come in. Skip and I go up on Main Street where I see Mark and Cindy Craig. He is the 28th Va. S.C.V. Commander and used to reenact with the 28th Va. Infantry Co. C Craig Mountain Boys. 51st members come up led by Capt. Pendleton. Other troops are about, also. When some Yankee Cav. show up, fighting erupts. I get some camcorder shots off. Lynell and I get lunch from the tent. The Davis girls come into camp. A siren announces the arrival of a long line of motorcycles that come through town.

Our rifles are inspected, and we form up in the parking lot. We have a company of ten when the Officers are included. We march to Main Street, Left Wheel, fire on Yank Cav., then leave. We come out onto the Town Park to fire on a battery and some cavalry. Later, the blue belly Infantry show up. After a Yank says, 'backwoods hick', I call him a 'blue belly city slicker'. Of course, I 'die' in the battle to save ammo. We clean rifles at camp. Back at Town Park, Lynell and I are first and second in line with our meal tickets. I register for the Martinsville event and we carry back some firewood to camp.

This is April 28, 2013, and last evening we took down our tent and made sleeping arrangements in back of our pickup under the camper shell. About 5:30 A.M. upon returning from the boat house facilities, I climb in back and hear rain drops. We are snug and have slept well the past two nights despite trains running nearby. Lynell goes up the street to bring back some breakfast. Someone has built a fire which burns in the rain. We spend a little time under the new 12x12 tent fly but go back to lie down in the pickup. Rain patters on the truck nearly putting me to sleep. The captain raps on the back window to let us know the rest of the event has been called off.

This is June 1, 2013, and I go to the Smith River Sports Complex where dozens of lacrosse players can be seen. At a different area, the Martinsville Reenactment is being held. Skip Fletcher comes in behind me at the registration tent. After we park, two golf carts pull up to wait on us, then give us a ride up to the site. I look for black powder to buy and buy the first I see. Later, I find some cheaper powder and buy two pounds of it. Seventeen-year locusts are about as I rest in the trees. I come out to talk with Allen Jackson thinking he might help me find some Confederates, but instead he introduces me to his new girlfriend.

Before the battle, I get up with Jim Wood. We were soldiers in the 28th Va. together, and it was his rifle that another soldier lost in Pickett's Charge at the 135th Anniversary of Gettysburg event. The 28th bought Jim another rifle. Jim, age 65 comes from the state of West Virginia and is a perfect gentleman.

Today we have a total force of 31 Confederates. I see ten Yankees including Skip but not counting their two cannon crews. We have two cannons, also. Jim serves on one of our crews today. There are not any cavalry present although the battle of Martinsville in April of 1865 was all cavalry. Jerry Hobbs writes my phone number on a bill, I think it is a 10-dollar bill, so he can further inform me concerning a cannon class.

This is Thursday June 27, 2013, and Lynell and I travel to Pennsylvania for the 150th Anniversary of the Battle of Gettysburg. We see a sign indicating the Borough of Gettysburg. We turn onto Confederate Avenue and I pull over to take pictures where Longstreet's Artillery had been. A pickup from Arkansas passes and a man in it wearing an upturned slouch hat gives a Rebel Yell. On up, we pull up and walk over to the Virginia Monument where reenactors of the 39th Georgia are posing.

We drive past more cannon and the tower Jud and I had climbed in 1996. At a motorcycle place, I get directions to Registration. We stand in line a while to get the wooden 'medallion' for this long-awaited event. Amid much confusion, we get going and turn off the hard top by the Sutlers. We drive through fields of parked vehicles before we ever see a tent. Once we ask for the whereabouts of Longstreet's Corps. I see Travis White's oldest daughter, all grown up now, then one of his sons and they direct us to camp. Officers Lester Harrell and Allen Jackson are up on the corner. Under threating skies Travis helps us set up our tent. We unload our stuff; afterward, on the way to park, see Provost Marshall Sammy Hughes.

I park twice before we walk to where I hear there are 60 Sutlers. On the way, a big pickup with bags of ice drops one. He is told but just drives on. I pick up the large bag and give it to a thankful Artillerist. Lynell buys a new dress, corset, and hat. I get paper tubes and a black tarred haversack. We enjoy some pulled pork barbeque. Henry Kidd has his art work on display and is also the Official Artist for this event. On walking back, we find a pink ribbon flying from our radio antenna and a 'tow this vehicle' sign on our windshield. We move down further away from the road. Joan is driving as she and Terry come by us. We help them set up on one side of us, Travis is on the other side. Captain Mike Pendleton calls for a meeting up by the fire. His wife Melissa and Officer Lester Harrell are present also. Later on, notes sound from the captain's fiddle.

On June 28, 2013, we are awakened at 5 A.M. after a good night's sleep, by the sound of distant drums. We must hurry to see if the Port-a-Johns are still in good working order. Someone starts the fire up, and soon I am cooking up some sausage patties. I get Terry to volunteer to take the last three pieces. I loan Provost Sammy Hughes, below a cup.

General Terry Shelton is the event overall Confederate Commander. I fill out two medical report sheets, one for the captain, and one for my haversack. This is my 119th event and I guess the first time for that.

The six of us that are the 51st Va. at this event: Captain Pendleton, Terry Williams, Travis White, Uriah White, Isaac White, and me march out and are joined by the 5th, 8th, 18th Co. G Virginia units and the 5th Texas. We all make up one company. I think back to the new Officers coat Capt.

Pendleton bought yesterday but is not wearing today. As part of my uniform, I am wearing a kepi and trousers of butternut jean cloth that once belonged to Sean Verlick, carrying the bullseye canteen purchased at the 135th Gettysburg, and wearing the black haversack I got last night. I wear the first 9-button grey shell jacket I ever had.

We form and march to a field to wait. Behind us, Officer Lester Harrell is holding the reins of a horse for a black Confederate lady sergeant to mount.

We march to another field to wait. General Bill Russell is riding a horse, probably the first time I've ever seen that. In the woods, we walk on a road, and we pass some Georgia tents. Slowly as we march further on, I realize we are now seeing Yankee tents. Thousands of Yankees line the dirt road here in the deep woods.

I hold my peace and stay out of trouble. We make a wrong turn down a hill, then we all take a break. I film some with the small camcorder. We march back up, turn left, and march through hundreds of Confederates lining the roadside. We come to a point

not far from the battlefield and are halted.

Now a good number of our Confederate troops march between us on the road. I use both of my cameras. We rest, some sleep, as the battle rages on the field. The captain lets me go over to the tree line to film the distant battle. I get a good variety of photos in the waiting area, too.

It is after 11 A.M. before we take the field. We are on high ground and have a commanding view of thousands of troops engaged in combat.

The panoramic view offers scenes of mass bodies of troops firing on each other, complete with cannons going off. In a battle line, we sweep down and across the field. Our flagbearer is in front of me, one man over to my right. Behind him is a 15-year-old boy in blue wearing a grey kepi from Pennsylvania. I hear him say a curse word followed by the word Yankee. We cross a ditch with water in it then have to fall back as fighting is at hand. A lot of 'buck tails' drop here. We cross over the ditch again and move through them. Terry is down and I think some of the White family. Our boys on both sides help out as we sweep the field of Yanks and push them back into their camp.

Travis is flanked by his sons Isaac and Uriah White. These men are descendants of Revolutionary War hero Officer Thomas Sumpter.

Victorious, we march back to camp to clean rifles. Lynell gets me some beef jerky. Capt. Pendleton and I carry bags of ice to camp. A medical emergency arises, again. An ambulance picks up Lester Harrell. Provost Sammy Hughes comes in the camp. After rain starts, Lynell falls asleep in our tent. I resupply my cartridge box, cap box, and fill the canteen. Capt. Mike and another man play fiddles. Lynell cooks up some chicken and rice. We have more time of wind and rain; some tents are even blown down. After the rain clears out, we get ready for battle. As before, we form up our big company at the dirt road. A man dressed as a Confederate but without a hat carries a big microphone, voice recorder, and a nice camera. I hear later, he's doing a story for a magazine article.

The man on the front rank in front of me, my file partner, starts telling some of the fellows about how at Spotsylvania, one time, a guy tackled their Color bearer, that he didn't 'get the memo'. I tell him I was the guy. He said that his Captain was mad! I said that I ought to know, I heard him cuss. He also said, "It was a great football tackle."

Eventually, we march down the hill into a large field and see Yanks massed along a distant creek. More of our boys join us. I film some cannon firing before we step off. The 28th Va. is on the field for this Battle of Culp's Hill. Barry Cornett, Leland Hedrick, Jeff Sobataka, and Bobby Compton are in there.

We do a lot of At the Oblique marching to get line. Right to the tree trees is a just under the stash of cases of water bottles. Travis White and his two boys dash in to bring some to us. From Travis, I get a 150th Gettysburg anniversary bottle of water souvenir. We are marched into the trees and fire on the Federals who are behind breastworks. It's a great fight and Capt. Mike lets me step back to film. The muzzle flashes grow brighter in the growing dusk. We march through woods as night catches us.

Some new folks are in camp and I loan out a jacket. Our Color bearer for the battle was the only lady in our unit and the only person, as far as we know, with an ancestor who fought in the Battle of Culp's Hill. I wear the black slouch hat I got at Gettysburg 19 years ago in 1994. The hat is older than the two on either side of me when we march into battle.

This is June 29, 2013, and the drums start at 6 A.M. Travis White starts the fire up and we get breakfast cooking. Colors are posted by Isaac and the 2 new guys. Lynell and I enjoy breakfast by the fire with Hannah, her father Travis, and her brothers, Uriah and Isaac. Rifles were cleaned before we ate and now Lynell cleans dishes. Joan Williams, Melissa Pendleton, and Hannah White are off; I think they will be attending a tea party somewhere. Soldiers accouter up and go out to a Longstreet Corps Dress Parade.

This is John Alger's first Parade and perhaps the largest number of troops ever in one place for the Corps. Generals Shelton and Russell address the Corps. I find myself on the front rank looking into the lens of a large camera pointed at me. I wish I could take a picture of the Corps at this moment. Someone comes forward to receive the Hillsman Scholarship Award. Back in camp, Lynell gets pictures of us.

Company Drill is conducted. We get lunch from the tent. A crowd gathers under the captain's tent fly as stories are told and old times relived. Skip Fletcher is at this event, as well, but he is with the Florida boys. Florida is the state Skip worked in and reenacted in for many years, and I hear was a high-ranking Officer there, too.

When I am resting in the tent, I hear the sounds of a distant battle raging. We are told to hurry up. Before long we are marching down the 'hill of death' as it is now called. People scurry to and from the water buffalo or big portable water tank, trying to fill canteens as the column of troops stops and starts periodically.

We stop by the Port-o-Johns and I get the whole column moving simply by placing my hand on a Port-o-John door handle. Our next stop is the big battlefield. The 'juice' has run out on my camcorder, so I use the Kodak camera to film and video. We rest in some trees, then march up behind a row of cannon. I film their fire, and after another of their volleys, we march through. We engage in rifle firing with hundreds of Yanks as hundreds more are coming to reinforce them. We cross a fence and stand in a gravel road firing when I take a 'hit' to end up against some piled up fence rails.

From here there is a magnificent scene of battle unfolding of which I get some photographs. Captain Pendleton shouts firing commands and hurries the boys to load. Sharp fighting ensues and Confederates push on more. The fighting ends prematurely due to some Officer's mistake.

About four scenarios were supposed to play out. We go back at 'the mosey' to clean rifles and eat. This was John Alger's first battle. At the tent across from our Captain's, Art celebrates his 53rd birthday. I am in charge of the detail that retires our company's Confederate Battle flag for the night. Its past 8:15 P.M., and a battle rages in the distance. Captain Pendleton fiddles the 'Bonnie Blue Flag.' On into the night, I hear laughter from the Capt.'s tent fly as Travis White tells another story.

This is June 30, 2013 and just after 5:30 A.M., I get up off my bent cot. I start carrying stuff out to the truck in the parking lot. Last evening, the Whites started carrying their equipment to the vehicle and they continue today. Back from the parking lot, I speak with Doug Camper. Yesterday, as well as today, I wear the 4-button sack coat I bought off his dad Pete 20 years ago, almost to the date. I get Lynell to go with me on the next trip. Up and down the 'hill of death' vehicles go as no guards are there to stop them. I hear one got stopped because he nearly ran over General Shelton. On the next two of my five trips, I get assistance from Travis and Uriah White. Coming back from my last trip, I see guards now out only letting Artillery or something they should get through. Now Lynell and the tent are at the pickup in the parking lot.

As I walk up the 'hill of death,' no hat or vest on and drenched in sweat, I meet Officer Harrell and some other Officers coming down the hill. I pass by the camp of the 28th Va., the unit I was here with at the 135th and I salute. In camp, the men are gone. From the supply tent I get my coat, my hat, my rifle, and accoutrements before joining the formation. We take a different route down the 'hill of death' to join other troops. We do some huge Wheels to get in place.

Henry Kidd explains to us how the real 'Rebel Yell' would have sounded: a high yelp, a deep whoop, and a loud youl, eehh, woup, youl. I believe the first and last parts are drawn out.

I think Henry will be portraying Armistead today in this Pickett's Charge reenactment. There is to be no talking or yelling as the charge moves across. For now, I Stack Arms. After a brief rest by a small creek and a free bottle of water, we Take Arms and move into the woods where thousands of Confederates are. We Stack Arms and lounge about. I take another picture of Travis and his boys. His daughter Hannah, wearing a green dress comes by; she is an 'Ice Angel.' There is a small praying mantis on our bayonets. Someone says, "He is praying for us." This calls for more pictures.

Hats are raised for the General Lee reenactor who rides in; chants of Lee, Lee, are heard.

Our 1ˢᵗ sergeant is a 19-year-old named Possum. We are Double-Quicked up to the field and step off. A good alignment is not held and it is not quiet; mostly 'give left' is heard and some get squeezed out of line.

We pass through the line of cannons. At a steep ditch with a wide marsh near a steep bank, I take my 'hit' and see water beneath my foot. I am 54 and across looking back at me is 56-year-old Terry Williams; with him is 17-year-old Isaac White. Isaac is only one of four of our combined company who gets to go over the wall today. I got to at the 135ᵗʰ and 145ᵗʰ Anniversary events!

I start back limping and try to take pictures discreetly. I stop at a caisson and am unaware at first that General Shelton and some of his staff are standing back a bit observing the charge.

As I continue back, I hear cheers and bugles. As hats are removed, I hold mine toward the scene as we have just honored and remembered in our on feeble way those brave Confederates of 150 years ago. The battle was really a draw as Lee stayed a whole day before he left Gettysburg.

The first person of the 51st I saw on arrival at this event was Hannah White, now she is the last person of the 51st I see before we leave.

I wish them good luck getting out of here. About 50 minutes after getting in the pickup we reach the hard surface road not far away. We turn and on the Emmitsburg Road cross through the path of the real Pickett's Charge of 150 years ago.

I have some notes from the 150th Anniversary Gettysburg event put on by the Blue Gray Alliance from June 27-30, 2013: My wife Lynell had two ancestors in the 38th Va. in Pickett's Charge; only those going over the wall in Pickett's Charge were instructed to load their rifles; John Alger suffered a sprained ankle in Pickett's Charge; more than one fifteen-year-old was in our company, once one was on either side of me; our rifles were inspected before every battle; I carried 225 rounds but shot only 47; one day Sgt. Shifty Williams shows me some passes he obtained somehow, now all he has to do is fill in the blanks; about 12,000 reenactors I hear were at the event. On another Note I've read the 135th held on the same grounds as the 150th event had 45,000 reenactors and Sutlers.

The Confederate Command Structure for the 150th Gettysburg follows; General Terry Shelton [Longstreet Corps] Commanding, First Corps General Barry Woods Commanding [Longstreet Corps], Surgeon Major Ranson Autry, 1st Div. Inf. Gen. Bill Russell [Longstreet Corps], 1st Brigade Col. Robert Stowe [Longstreet Corps], 1st Battalion Col. Tim Smith [Longstreet Corps], 2nd Battalion Col. Ray Pickett [Longstreet Corps], 3rd Battalion Col. Steve Haden [Longstreet Corps], 4th Battalion Col. Thomas Tarkenton [Longstreet Corps], 5th Battalion Col. Chris Burns [Georgia Division], 2nd Brigade Gen. Ken Whitt [Jackson's Corps], 1st Battalion Col. Duffie Miller [Jackson's Corps 5th Reg.], 2nd Battalion Col. Bryan Boyle [Southern Legion Jackson's Corps], 3rd Battalion Col. N. E. Miller [Wise's Legion/Jackson's

Corps], Second Corps General Joe Way Commanding [Cleburne's Division], Cleburne's Division Gen. Duane Hamby, Kings Division General Jack King, Huckabee's Division Gen. William Huckabee, Southern Division General Chris Anders Artillery Commander, General Craig McCann [Longstreet Corps] Cavalry Commander, Brevet General Micky Helms [Longstreet Corps].

This is the evening of September 6, 2013, and Lynell and I arrive in Franklin County at the Lake Watch Plantation for their Civil War Days. Robert and Terry help us set up. I give Lynell money to buy me a straw hat that caught my eye. This is also my youngest son Michael's 25th birthday.

This is the morning of September 7, 2013, and I go to see if a Port-o-John is in good working order. I see the red lights glowing from the top of Bojangles. After daylight the voice of Skip Fletcher booms out instructions. I go up for biscuits from Bojangles and carry Lynell her breakfast. The 60th Va. post Colors as we salute. Acting Captain Allen Jackson has Sgt. Williams, Cpl. Brown, and me engage in rifle drill when Skip drives up with Confederate Commander Lester Harrell. Later Bremen, the Davis family, Chuck, Carol, and Leon come in. Leon is wearing an antibiotic stint harness. I get pictures of two-star-wearing Officer Harrell holding his new granddaughter.

We go out to drill and see the 28th Va. come out also. We see Captain Pendleton who has had recent knee surgery being driven by in a golf cart. Acting Capt. Jackson sharpens up the 51st on its marching and rifle drill. A State Trooper from Glade Hill is interested in joining up. We have lunch and a time of fellowship; I show Gettysburg pictures.

It's time to get accoutered up and formed up. I assist in stacking of arms. We are Color Company and Miss Lil with fresh wet black powder on her face is our Color bearer.

We engage the nine Yankees and I give some rounds to Ben Davis before a cannon goes off and I go down. After the battle we march in review and clean rifles. We walk up to eat supper under the big tent. A stop on the way back at Heirloom Emporium sutler. Terry, Robert, and I retire Company Colors. The Lone Ivy String Band is playing under the big tent.

This is September 8, 2013, and Lynell walks up the hill to return with some Bojangles' biscuits for another free breakfast. Some of the Harrells join us in camp from the hotel they stayed in last night. Lively conversation abounds under the trees at our camp. Some have gone up the hill for Church under the big tent, Lynell's stomach is not feeling well. Captain Bremen Harrell conducts a drill. We are down from the dozen soldiers that comprised our company yesterday.

Another recruit prospect comes in camp. Now come three others. We get uniform items together with rifles, leathers, and so on for them. I contribute two coats, some 100 caps, and a cap box. 1ˢᵗ Sgt. Williams and Cpl. Brown instruct the new guys in drill. George Davis and Doug Camper join us for the battle; our number is over a dozen today. The 28ᵗʰ Va. opens up the battle with an ambush. The Yankees consist of a company and at least one mounted cannon. Our Cavalry charge around them to change over to fight us with the rest of the galvanized Yanks. We burn a lot of powder but I stick this one out. At the end, we advance as skirmishers into the Yanks. I cross rifles with one until he 'dies'. We march in review to a cheering crowd. 'Gen. Lee' gave us a speech before the battle and now Commander Lester Harrell, with those two stars on his collar, gives us a parting one.

This is October 4, 2013, and I arrive here at the birthplace of Major General James Ewell Brown Stuart at Ararat, Virginia, very close to the state of North Carolina. I pass through registration and Susan Hill helps me set up the tent. Terry Williams and I load firewood on the pickup at 'Ft. Marvin'. I give him and Robert Brown a ride to the Sutlers where I buy a shirt before parking the pickup by the road. Jerry Trent III arrives and Terry and I instruct him in drill. I go up on Laurel Hill; Gene Fain and Sonny Spence from our S.C.V. are here. We set up the tent fly.

This is October 5, 2013, and Jerry Trent and I stayed in the tent last night. He gets up early and chops firewood. Terry, Robert, and I post Company Colors. Allen Jackson gets us out to drill. After breakfast, we have to hurry up and wait. Eventually, we make it up Laurel Hill to engage in Battalion drill lead by General Shelton, then break up into Company drill. We Stack Arms to mill about the Sutlers a bit. I get two of 'The Truth concerning the Confederate Battle Flag' C.D.s from the Mt. Airy S.C.V. camp. Our Wharton-Stuart S.C.V. are set up beside them with Kenneth Holt, Mike Corns, and others here.

I guard some stacked rifles as they march off to raise the giant 2nd National Confederate flag in the flag raising ceremony. Judson is on the detail this year. I grab a cheeseburger from the Ararat Rescue Squad. Lynell arrives in camp wearing her new dress. Allen Jackson's parents bring the banana pudding that has become a tradition at this event. We march up the road to cut across the hill to stage for battle. The 51st Virginia Infantry Company D is comprised of fifteen members set to face the foe. We are engaging the Yankees when our General Shelton is 'hit,' which makes us mad. We lose Bremen and others. We charge and, in front of me, one of our State Troopers Jonathan Clark is 'hit.' I am giving the Rebel Yell, and at battle's end, Larry Mabe and I are facing their boy flag bearer. We all Pass in Review. Jud is helping man the Wharton-Stuart S.C.V. Camp #1832 table, Jonathan was using his rifle. We have a rifle cleaning time at camp. Jerry and I go to the Sutlers. I meet Mark Thompson of Judson's High School graduating class. I buy supper and a pair of suspenders. Robert Brown walks using a cane.

This is the morning of October 6, 2013, and Jerry Trent went home last night without telling me so naturally I was worried. Terry let me know this morning. I busy myself in carrying stuff to the truck. Our Colors are posted before the 1st Kentucky posted theirs today. We then get ready for Dress Parade. 2nd Sgt. Harrell is awakened by his mom but remains in his tent until after Dress Parade. After parade, Jonathan Wilson, a long-time reenactor, joins us. He is in the next picture.

Allen Jackson has Church Call with an overflowing crowd under Captain Pendleton's tent fly.

After church service, a Company Meeting is conducted. Joan Williams will draw the quilt raffle after the battle. Leon Craft sees a long black snake near the parking lot. Later, Jerry Trent comes in and uses Jud's rifle and leathers (another word for accoutrements) today. On this hot sweaty day, the fighting is in the form of a tactical or unscripted battle. Jonathan Wilson and I are sent out as scouts. Jonathan even goes up to the Yankee camp. Later, we go over near the Ararat River and up a hill. Elements of the 1st Kentucky and our boys of the 51st

Va. move up in the woods on this hill. Terry, Bremen, and I see Yanks converging between us and our men on the field. We shoot into their flanks, and I even get behind some. I am wearing my 'bubba teeth' when we 'Pass in Review.' Jerry and I help load up S.C.V. things before we leave.

This is Saturday, October 19, 2013, and I help out with a Confederate Grave Marker Dedication. I arrive on this overcast day behind the Patrick County High School where I graduated in 1977 and where Lynell teaches now. I go to a house at the end of a dirt road where a friendly dog named Clay jumps on me. I wait awhile for someone to tell me if a graveyard is around, but finally I leave.

At the school road is Gene Reamey and his cannon here from Henry County. Other members of the Stuart-Hairston S.C.V. Camp #515 begin to arrive. I will be the only representative of the Wharton-Stuart S.C.V. Camp #1832. A big Chevy 4-wheel drive pickup pulling a trailer and a 4-wheeler are the only vehicles that make it to the graveyard nearly at the top of a mountain. About 40 people are finally in place. The man who rode up on the back of the pickup with me

has a grand and great grandfather buried here. This new marker is for Private William Isaiah Craddock of Company H, 58th Virginia Infantry.

Pat and Gene Reamey, William is Pat's ancestor.

Page | **229**

His history is given, we fire volleys, and "Taps" is played as part of the Ceremony. In my early years of wearing the uniform, I was involved in numerous grave marker dedications but I never kept a count of them as I did with the reenactments.

This is November 1, 2013, and Lynell and I arrive here at Ft. Branch near Hamilton, N.C. We pay $20.00 a piece for walk-on registration which includes Saturday meals. At the Regimental Quartermaster, I get a lock-plate screw and caps. We park as the rain starts.

Rain falls off and on during the night. We sleep in back of the truck under the camper shell. I put in a new leather shoestring in one of my brogans. We have breakfast from the food we brought. I put in the new lock-plate screw on my 3-band Enfield Armisport rifle that I had with me 20 years ago at this place. I go for a walk about the camps, the cabins, the fort, the museum, and the sutlers; I take photos of soldiers drilling. The skies are becoming more overcast.

I get accoutered up and go over to the Confederate camp and meet Ken Meador of the 28th Va. The other three men of the unit at this event come back from the Sutlers. Soon, we go join a company comprised of parts of companies with the 12th Va. as its core. Today, I am honored to have Henry Kidd as my Captain.

Gary Elliott, from Danville, Virginia, is my file partner; he lives just off of Westover Drive where I lived in the mid to late 1960's.

We are marched out to Fort Branch; the earthen fort overlooks the Roanoke River far below. Our skirmishers in the field are driven in by galvanized North Carolinians. We fire from our moat wall awhile, then fall back to fire over the earthen fort walls.

Now we fall back into the interior of the fort, soon Yankees are inside exchanging gunfire. We give the Rebel Yell as we advance on them to end the battle. I take pictures and Lynell videos from a far. Later, I clean on the rifle as Lynell reads and sleeps. We walk over early for the meal, and I buy another 'Gettysburg 135th Photographic Review', published by 'The Civil War News'. At the meal that is served, we have barbeque, venison, potatoes, green beans, and bread. When we get back to the pickup truck, I find I left the door open but the two rifles are still here. We hear drum and fife music for a long time after it gets dark. Several times, the truck vibrates from the fort cannon firing, which is a good distance from where we are parked.

We have three beeswax candles we bought from a guy who was making them last evening. He uses the money for school history programs. At 3:45 A.M., we leave out and see the sun coming up over the Atlantic Ocean at Nags Head, N.C. At Chesapeake, Va., we visit my son Michael, our daughter-in-law Rebecca, and granddaughter Abby. We get back home to make it a 748-mile round trip.

On Saturday, November 23, 2013, I attend another Martinsville Christmas Parade. It has been years since the last one I was in. I remember marching with the 42nd Va. reenactors in that one. In this one, we ride on a 'float.' I find the Stuart-Hairston S.C.V. camp's entry then I go back to return from the car with my hat, rifle, and accoutrements. A woman drives a truck pulling a trailer with nine Confederate soldiers and one cannon on it. Three are from the Rockingham Rangers S.C.V. camp. There are many entries in the parade, and there are many people watching the parade. I say, 'Merry Christmas!'

This is Saturday, December 7, 2013, and time for this year's Stuart Christmas Parade. Lynell and I prepare; I wear my brogans, black wool trousers, a grey nine-button shell jacket, and butternut color kepi. I bring my rifle, accoutrements, two pair of white gloves, and a pair of 'gators.' Lynell has on a pretty dress and the new hat she bought at the 150th Gettysburg event. We go across the road from Moody's Funeral Home where we always stage for the parade. Brother Judson is here to 'call the shots,' and another younger brother, David, comes over to see us. I give him my Kodak camera because he will be watching the parade down on Main Street. Sonny Spence has his pickup, trailer, and bales of hay. When our time comes to step off, two members of the camp carry the Wharton-Stuart Sons of Confederate Veterans Camp #1832 banner between them.

Next comes Kenneth Holt carrying the Confederate Battle flag and members with rifles march behind him. Behind us comes the truck and float. At our Courthouse with a Confederate statue, we attempt to shoot a volley but only about half the guns go off. We have fourteen people in all.

On December 14, 2013, the Wharton- Stuart S.C.V. Camp #1832 holds its Annual Christmas Banquet at the Reynolds Homestead in Critz, Virginia. We carry the food with us that Lynell has prepared including a roast, potatoes, baked beans, broccoli-cauliflower casserole, deviled eggs, a relish tray, and a pie. A soft drink and rolls come with us also. We have twelve in attendance counting Mrs. Brown's baby, due in January.

CHAPTER 9 - 2014

This is February 1, 2014, and also the date of this year's meeting of the 51st Virginia Infantry Company D. Lynell and I arrive at the new house of the Robert Brown family in Patrick Springs, Virginia. Captain Mike Pendleton greets us and helps us unload the food we brought that Lynell prepared. The baked beans, broccoli-cauliflower casserole, rolls, cookies, and coconut pies are added to the food already here. More people come in and we eat. A total of 26 people is present. The meeting is held upstairs. Mike Pendleton goes back in as Captain.

Allen Jackson will be taking on more preaching duties at his church and will not be able to join us as much this year. Terry Williams goes in as 1st Sgt. and Robert Brown as the 2nd Sgt. Events voted on for our company are Cloyd's Mountain, New Market, Trevilian Station, Thunder in the Valley, J.E.B. Stuart, and Cedar Creek. I plan on going a day up to Franklin County Civil War Days. The Camp of the Instruction is voted on to be a one-day thing at the J.E.B. Stuart Birthplace on March 8th. I pay $125.00 for dues, insurance, and registration for some events. A portion of all fund monies raised will go to the Longstreet Corps Scholarship Fund. The company has sets of leathers and rifles to help out newcomers at events.

This is March 15, 2014, and the day the 51st Va. is holding its Camp of the Instruction at the J.E.B. Stuart Birthplace.

Last week, the event was not held due to snow. When I get to the birthplace at 8 A.M., I am met by the company Officers who said, they saw me earlier at Hardees. I hear Lester is getting out of reenacting. Leon arrives from Roanoke; he had a GPS problem. Some of us go down to the small main building. Robert

gets a sweatshirt for his brother's birthday. Feathers, chicken manure, and smell is scattered about for fertilizer. Up near the big flagpole, Captain Pendleton marches us out and we Stack Arms and drill. A lot of time is spent on the J thing drill movement. We come down to a pavilion for a brief break and a 'new guy' drives up in his shiny full-size Chevrolet pickup. His name is Glennis Young and the 54-year-old lives in Franklin County at Boones Mill. Now we go back up the hill to drill without and with the rifles we never fired.

This is April 2, 2014, and I have arrived on site at the New River Valley Fairgrounds for the 150th Anniversary Battle of Cloyd's Mountain. I see 2nd Sgt. Brown, Capt. Pendleton, and Pvt. Craft. I have to turn down the Capt. when he asks, would I be 1st Sgt. Behind me is Travis White with right many folks, He will accept the captain's offer. I go over to register and see Travis and Isiah's names on a list of soldiers making the road march tomorrow. I stop in on Sutler Row but see no port-o-Johns. At camp, the Officers return from a meeting. Officer Doug Camper and members of the 60th Va. Company K come in and I will keep 3 of their rifles in my tent.

This is April 5, 2014, and the Battle of Cloyd's Mountain which was originally fought on May 9, 1864 but, due to a conflict with another reenactment this year, is being held this weekend. I sleep off and on during the night in the tent here in Pulaski County, Virginia. The last flame flickers from the candle in my

Lantern before I go out and still cannot find a Port-o-John. The boys of the 60th Va. lay straw on the ground where some of them will be sleeping.

I dream I see my Grandson Oron. The 60th posts Colors as I take pictures with Doug's camera. The few of the 51st here form with the 60th. Colonel Pendleton speaks to us on a few things we need to know.

Officer Camper shuffles us about before we are ready for Dress Parade. I wear the old trousers and 4-button sack coat of Doug's Dad Pete in honor of their ancestors who fought here. Our hands and feet are freezing in the cold wind. Jeff Sobataka is the Parade Adjutant. Afterwards, those going on the march leave, including Travis, Uriah, and Isaac White. The wind blew hard all night and is still blowing cold today. Acting 1st Sgt. Robert Brown is doing a good job at his temporary position.

Joan Williams awaits the arrival of her husband Terry. He comes in and then comes George and Sam Davis. We board the Pulaski County school buses to the battlefield. I hear Pulaski County spent 20,000 dollars on this event. On our way, we pass the Confederate soldiers on their five-mile march. With us is the only member of the 1st Ky. present. I get George to use my camera to photograph from his window the Battle of Cloyd's Mountain Historical Marker. We disembark and I stack seven rifles before we go in waiting mode. There is a 500-year-old tree on the battlefield with mini balls still embedded in it.

Cloyd's farm can be seen on another hill. Robert, George, Sam, and I enjoy a snack from my haversack. The 36th Va. is here as a unit as they were in 1864. The 28th Va. combines with other units to form the 45th Va. We are in the center with the 60th Va. who were also in this 1864 battle.

An informative talk is given before we step off up a knoll. A cannonade has started the battle already. Spectators are on the distant hill near a house. To our left, past the Yankee cannon, are troops under the trees. Leon Craft is on the Color detail with the 60th Va. Colors. We come up on a long line of rotten log breastworks. The 28th Va. go out as skirmishers. Captain Lawhorn takes a gruesome looking 'hit.' Soon, Colonel Mike Pendleton is barking out firing commands. The Yankees I am firing at number more than our men. I take a 'hit' over the top rail. One of Travis's boys is sprawled over on the Yankee's side of the fence. George Davis is one of those taking a massive 'hit'. To my immediate left he goes over as logs go down, I see cartridges spilling out of his box. The battle rages on and turns into 'hand to hand' combat as we are over run. When the battle is over, I see Travis on the ground to my front. Officer Doug Camper is laying just behind me. He had seven ancestors who fought here. Then I see 2nd Sgt. Robert Brown who is a real casualty, he has a bloody spot above his left eye having been hit by a falling rail.

 Colonel Pendleton and the 60th flag bearer escaped off the field and escaped capture.

We clear weapons before the ride back. Some of the ladies made it out to watch the battle. On the ride back, I speak with Mark Minter of Danville, Va., and we get caught up on old times. The 150th Civil War Anniversary tractor trailer is here at the Fairgrounds. When I am cleaning my rifle, a man who lives nearby and has his two kids with him stops to talk with me. I go up on the Fairground and get supper from a mobile kitchen. Coming by the five Sutlers I get six candles. Daniel Young the Blacksmith gives me his card when I tell him about our Camp for Kids planned for September. He may bring the cannon. In camp, I show Travis, Uriah, and Hannah the Gettysburg material I have. The next camp over, we hear the 28th Va. retiring their Company Colors.

This is April 6, 2014, and I spend the night on the Pulaski County Fairgrounds once again in my tent. Leon Craft has the tent next to mine and he says, "He went walking in the night." I think the older gentleman looks 'fit as a fiddle'. I hear Officers conversing by the fire before it is light. Various ones are getting breakfast. Travis White's youngest child, his 9-year-old daughter, Destiny, is here for her first event. I see her eating cereal as her dad often does. 2nd Sergeant Brown has our rifles inspected and two or three fail. Colonel Pendleton, our Brigade Commander, has us march out for Dress Parade as I hear the Rev. Alan Farley sounding Church Call. I take pictures of Travis White wearing his 'bubba teeth,' soon he is on his cell phone calling in one of his cousins to the event.

At the Dress Parade Overall Confederate Commander Will Perkinson and his Adjutant Jeff Sobataka are recognized for their weekend service with nice books of historical value. The hosts for this event are outstanding.

After the parade, the dirty rifles are cleaned and Travis's cousin makes it here. This is his first reenactment. Where we wait to board the buses, more people are recognized, one called forward is a local man with the last name of Sutherlin, three cheers are given. Like yesterday, we disembark at the battlefield, stack arms, and wait. Pictured below is Dave Lawhorn and Jeff Sobataka.

We enjoy lounging about and I get some more photos. We march up on the hillside and stop. The Artillery has been dueling, and now the two top Confederate Commanders reenact an argument that Jenkins and McCausland had. We go into the rotten log breastworks and the 28th men deploy as skirmishers again with Lawhorn taking 'hit's'. Before the battle, my ole 1st Sgt. and I had exchanged handshakes and a hug. After they rejoin our ranks, the 36th Va. goes out to engage the Yanks. More of them come on from the bottom of the hill now. With one of my first 'shots,' I see their Color bearer go down. I take a 'hit' and am dragged away from the fence. Soon we are being overrun by the Federals. I sneak out my camcorder to film and cannot believe all the great action I'm getting until I see the lens cap is still on. We clear weapons, board buses, and return. I am packed up and about to leave when I look up to see another small plane. We saw quite a few this weekend as the airport is just across the way.

Officer Doug Camper pictured below remembers his 7 soldier ancestors who fought here at this battle.

This is April 12, 2014, and Confederate Memorial Day is being observed here in Patrick County at the old Courthouse in Stuart, Virginia. Kenneth Holt is the Wharton-Stuart Sons of Confederate Veterans camp #1832 Commander and he introduces the guest speaker who is a former camp Commander, Chris Washburn. Before he delivers his speech, he reads a proclamation from S.C.V. Headquarters that I gave him which denounces the Klan and other hate groups. Rockingham Ranger camp member Jerry Hobbs is here with some other N.C. folks. A few feet away, a guy is pouring concrete from a wheelbarrow as improvements to the property are being made. Just before our first volley, Pat Reamey of the Stuart-Hairston S.C.V. Camp #515 arrives.

He was at the Spencer Penn Center with his camp today at a B.B.Q. contest and other things going on. We probably averaged 25 people at the event as some came and went.

This is May 16, 2014, and we have arrived at New Market, Virginia, for the 150th Anniversary Battle of New Market. First, we stop at registration up by the Museum. We get passes and some gold looking coins as event souvenirs. There is an Honor Guard at the Museum entrance for guests who are arriving in all their finery.

We drive past the Sutlers and up on a hill see Captain Pendleton who directs us to camp and helps us set up our tent. We see John Alger and some ladies that are with him. Travis and his son Isaac White walk up, as does Robert Brown. I speak with Leon Craft, also. Skip and Beverly Fletcher are on site. The Captain, Robert, and Skip go with

me as my 2000 ZR2 S10 Chevrolet pickup is commandeered for a firewood run. Travis builds the fire.

The fellows set up the tent fly, and I park the truck, and then meet Lynell at the Sutlers. Before it rains, we purchase a 3-prong fork, two corks, two shoe laces of rawhide, two 'Harpers Weekly' reproduction Journal's, socks, a corset, a shirt, and a book on the 'Eighth Georgia Regiment'. At the tent, Lynell gets a call from her brother Billy, a childhood friend of mine, who she once dated, has lost his battle with cancer. His name is James Reynolds. The rain continues to fall.

     This is May 17, 2014, and by the moonlight, we go to 'check out' the not so far away Port-o-Johns. With the Sutlers just down the hill and the parking not so far away, this is the best camp we've ever had at New Market!

     Travis White is cooking bacon over the fire to go with the sausage he already has cooked up. Lynell gives me two frying pans of food to put on the fire grate. Skip is on the Color Detail and posts our new Virginia State flag for the first time. 'First Call' comes, then 1st Sgt. Terry Williams forms company, and the 51st Va. takes the field. Our company is Color Company. A Color Guard is formed of eight noncommissioned officers, Skip, and Joe from the 60th Va., go into the Color Guard. We have a Dress Parade using Hardee's manual of arms. Longstreet Corps is not here for this event. In one of the longest period's I can recall of drill, we do Company Drill, Battalion Drill, then more Company Drill.

I buy a two-dollar seven-pound bag of ice. Lynell and I get our picture taken with the new flag. I photograph the flag bearer of the Virginia flag for this event in the Color guard. His ancestor was a 51st Va. flag bearer. He is a 24th Va. reenactor and his dog tent is set up across the company street from us.

Lynell and I go to Sutler row. Nearby I happen upon a Yankee Artillery demonstration. Lynell gets a cape, a pencil box, and chalk board. I eat lunch in the tent. The 51st gets First Call, and, when we get on the field, Stack Arms. 2nd Sgt. Brown and Pvt. Craft are chosen to guard the stacks of arms as we wait. The captain's tent fly, set up this side of the fire pit, now has soldiers seeking shade under it.

The traffic from Interstate 81 can be seen and heard from our vantage point. The Battalion takes arms, marches up the hill, then does a By Files Left. Marching through the woods at times, we come out at the dome shaped Museum. We have another Stack Arms and Rest session. The Artillery and the Cavalry have a go at it. Now on top of the hill, we see the spectators as specks in the distance. We get to fire and advance. Isaac White goes down and something red that really looks like blood is coming out of his mouth. I think what a pity the spectators are so far away.

The Virginia State flag goes down many times but is picked up. I am next to the Color guard and there are times when the flag brushes me; I hold my fire when the wind is whipping it in front of me. Once when a cannon is fired at us, Skip takes a painful 'hit' and howls piteously. I see George Davis and Travis get 'shot'. George and son Sam arrived today just before drill. Now we press the Yanks and have them on the move. Captain Pendleton has about three soldiers of Company D left when the bugle sounds ending the battle. I see a black Confederate soldier walk by. We march back after clearing weapons. Some good humor exchanges take place between the left-and-right wing Commanders before we are dismissed.

A big rifle cleaning session is in full swing. Lynell cooks chili. During the battle, Melissa Pendleton took good battle pictures for me with my camera which I now view. Lynell and I go to the Bushong House to get our picture taken. She goes back to camp and I go to the restroom up by the Museum to charge my camcorder battery. Lynell is the sponsor of the Civil War Reenactment Club where she teaches at Patrick County High School. The film I am making is to be shown to the club. I film some cannon night firing in the field by the Museum on my way back to camp with some of the Davis family.

This is May 18, 2014, and during the night, Lynell jolts me out of a nightmare I am having. I calm down and then pray for the kids and grandkids. It drops to 44 degrees and now the company fire is ringed with men. Travis White tosses in an empty cereal box as he munches cereal. Lynell gives me a frying pan of a breakfast medley to put on the fire grate. I help her put on the new corset and now she wears her dress instead of her new skirt; she had problems with the drawstring on the new piece of clothing. I let Leon take my place on the Color Detail; he and Connor post the two flags at the tent fly. Ken Meador of the 28th Va. will be with us today as he was yesterday. He has a new tent which he acquired yesterday by selling or trading his old one. His wife Susie and her beagle service dog are here, too. After the Dress Parade, there is no drill today. Men of the 51st Va. assemble for pictures at the Bushong House. The ladies including

Melissa, Lynell, Joan, and Beverly eventually join us. The flag bearer, whose ancestor was a 51st Va. flag bearer, and Color Guard members are here.

Years ago, the 51st reenactors had pictures made here. And 150 years ago, the 51st Va. was a force to be reckoned with on the field of battle behind this house. Travis and I are wearing Bubba teeth at times and he can be seen looking out a few of the windows, at times. Later, some of us assemble under the tent fly to hear Robert Brown deliver a sermon from the Old Testament, to go with the praying and singing we have. Lynell and I eat and take trips carrying stuff to the pickup before I am confined to camp at 12 noon.

We accouter up and march out. Isaac White shares the 'red blood makeup' with me. Some is placed on the hand that was shot with the musket I now carry. After our weapons are inspected, we have to load and shoot at high elevation then shoot up a bunch of caps. Up the hill, we take the same route to the Museum as yesterday. Today, it looks like the whole Confederate Army is here. Cannons are to our front, then the Cavalry passes to the front. Lots of stacked arms are about. Skip Fletcher meets up with some ole Florida friends.

A soldier gets on a wall to read and pray. Cannons fire before he can finish. A call to arms, today we are known as the 51st Virginia Battalion. We move up on line to move through the cannon and attack the Yankees. Now marching between the big barn and the Bushong house, we see off to our right the V.M.I. Cadets passing by the back of the house on this sunny day with sky of fluffy white clouds. In the Peach Orchard, I take my 'hit' because the month of February is called out, a prearranged sign for this battle for when the month of one's birth is called. What this also means to me is that now I am free to sneak in some filming. I get behind a peach tree after the battle line has moved on to continue. John Alger's daughter's friend gives me some cold water to drink from a cup. The real young man at the tree also gets special attention. As the battle is ending, I see Frank Mosley rise up from the grass about 40 yards over. The 'dead' and 'wounded' rejoin their units. Our Commanders commend us for a good job and we Pass in Review. We are marched back, I change clothes, take down the tent, and get in the long line leaving. I could argue this was our best New Market event from a reenactors point of view.

This is May 24, 2014, and I once again make a journey to Ararat, Va., here in Patrick County to the birthplace of Major General James Ewell Brown Stuart. This is albeit a one-time event as I join with others to mark the 150th year of the General's passing. Tents are set up. Mrs. Shirley Keene, Director of the J.E.B. Stuart Birthplace Preservation Trust, is officiating, I believe.

I enjoy the free lunch of B.B.Q., slaw, beans, potatoes, roll, and a soda. Captain Mike Pendleton is on fiddle, Larry Mabe is on banjo, and they are aided by a Mr. Conner in bringing forth music to our ears. There are displays set up, and I think J.E.B. Stuart the fourth is one of the guests. Captain Pendleton calls the commands when the volleys are fired by him, Judson, Larry, Terry, a dismounted Cavalryman, and me. A J.E.B. Stuart impersonator speaks. We Present Arms as Marvin Keen does not miss a note playing 'Taps' on his electronic bugle. I stop by the captain's house on my way home so he can download the New Market video and pictures.

This is June 7, 2014, and I participate in the 4th Annual Battle of Martinsville, Va., put on by the Stuart-Hairston Camp #515 Sons of Confederate Veterans of Martinsville, Virginia. Lynell and I arrive at the backside of the Smith River Sports Complex in Henry County. They let us in for free and give us a golf cart ride up from the parking lot. A man who works for Daniel Young the Blacksmith extracts a cleaning patch from the barrel of my musket for me. I get up with some Confederate troops then go back to the Blacksmith/Sutler tent of Daniel Young's; I buy a pound of FFF black powder. He will also narrate the upcoming battle. Jim Wood is here from West Virginia for the event. I show the veteran reenactor my video and pictures from New Market. There are cannons but no horses here. The Confederate force numbers seventeen. I was the last rifle toting Confederate to hit the ground. I told Doug Camper in a Federal uniform to 'stab' me. An officer and two flag bearers survive.

This is June 20, 2014, and I arrive just before dark somewhere in Virginia for the 150th Anniversary battle of Trevilian Station.

At registration, I am the only one for a while so I just park on the dirt road. In camp, I spot Beverly Fletcher, then the men who have gone for firewood arrive. I help Skip, Robert, Ken, and the captain unload the firewood. I have a dog tent with me but I just go to the parking lot to sleep in back of the truck under the camper shell. Soon it is raining again.

This is the morning of June 21, 2014, and I get accoutered up and walk to the camp of the 51st Va. Skip and Beverly have their grandson here. I hand out some 8X10's and 4X6 pictures from New Market. Ken Meador is kind enough to give me some coffee that goes in my big old cup.

1st Sgt. Williams and 2nd Sgt. Brown flank Pvts. Fletcher and Meador in the posting of Company Colors.

Leon Craft comes in and deposits some items in the supply tent. A bugler plays 'Dixie.' We march out to Dress Parade and see General Shelton, our Corps Commander, has shaved some whiskers and lost some weight, also. The 2013 Soldier

of the Year Award is given out along with some promotions. We have Battalion Drill then a lengthy Company Drill. There are only seven of the 51st and most of us go over to check out the four Sutlers; we then go to the grounds of an old house complete with, out buildings. An Abe Lincoln impersonator shakes our hands.

Robert and I get B.B.Q. sandwiches. I buy a $10.00 event medallion and order a video being made of this event. Joan and Terry Williams are here with us as is Capt. Pendleton. We enjoy talking with Officer Bill Russell, one of my favorite people. He has his own 'capture the flag' story. I take pictures of a General Lee impersonator. A Cavalry battle has started in a nearby field. Ken and Susie Meador and their friendly beagle are pictured below.

I hear 150 years ago; this was indeed a large-scale clash of cavalry. My cartridge box has 60 rounds of ammo. Earlier, I bought two bags of 48 rounds each from Mike Broome of the 1st Ky.; now we march out to join the rest of Longstreet Corps. Officer Bobby Compton of the 28th Va. inspects my rifle. Earlier in the day, I had given him an 8X10 from Cloyd's Mountain. We follow Gen. Shelton and his Staff, who are on horseback, across the dirt road, into a field to Stack Arms, and wait. Capt. Pendleton orders 1st Sgt. Williams and me to help move a cannon and its limber to another part of the field. Our cannon on a hill behind us, open up. We are up next to the crowd.

Barry Woods commands our wing and Bill Russell the other wing as we advance toward the Yanks. I fire a few rounds. Their Cavalry come in firing pistols rapidly and I take a 'hit.' Ken and I were 'shot' down close to each other and after the battle rejoin the others. As I lie on the field, I hear the announcer say, 'In England a Civil War Reenactor has to intern 10 years as a Yankee before he can become a Confederate soldier." One young soldier went through the battle with a 'Go Pro' strapped to his head, and back across the road now, he returns it to the photographer who got him to wear it.

I clean my rifle while sitting under a tree. Robert Brown takes my cup over to the house with the big porch for free lemonade. A lady comes by and tells of free rations for soldiers. Low and behold, Robert returns with some in a handkerchief. Our ladies provided us with cooling cloths to put around our necks. The day so far has been overcast and hot. Leon had to leave after the battle and planned on getting a medallion on his way out. Terry, Joan, Robert, and I walk over to the area of the old house. Many are the Cavalry and a few infantry that go up the dirt road to some special event being held. Before dark, I witness a real wedding held in a Cavalry camp.

This is June 22, 2014, and another good night was spent in the back of the pickup. I take gear to stage it in the supply tent at camp. Terry, Robert, and I go over to the food area to get breakfast. After Longstreet Corps Headquarters Post Colors, then we can post ours. The same four of yesterday post Colors today. We

go over to the camp of the 1st Ky. I get 100 caps from Mike Broome. We join them for Dress Parade. There is no music for the parade and I don't recall any yesterday. Afterwards, we see Glennis Young and his wife are here. He will replace Leon so now we have our company again. Terry, Robert, and I are on our way back over to the old house and pass the Gen. Lee impersonator's tent; he and ole Abe sat talking together.

Robert and Terry get free rations and lemonade at the porch of the old house, from the ladies that are here. Skip and his grandson are here as well. A Pentecostal Holiness Preacher is giving Church Call on the lawn under the big trees. He can play a guitar and sing as well as preach. My Dad, Terry E. Leviner, who passed on in 1995 was a Pentecostal Holiness Preacher as was my wife Lynell's dad, Willie B. Jones.

I go back for my camera so I can video a portion of the service. Back at camp, the new guy Glennis Young receives more instruction in drill from our 1st and 2nd Sergeants. His wife looks the part of a lady of the mid 1860's. We form up into a reduced Corps of about 55 down from the 130 something of yesterday. We go out to await battle and I get to Stack Arms. After the battle opens, we are marched up near the spectators to start driving back some Federals. Our Cavalry get involved, and we reattach to the Color Company to continue firing. It's a rather quick, sharp battle.

We are marched across the road and are told to be ready to go in about 40 minutes. I clean on my rifle as I had poured water down the hot barrel, not knowing we would be put back in. I get some food in me, too. Soon we have formed up again.

Ken Meador standing behind me says that he can see the General through the hole in my hat. Years ago, I cut out the hole to the size of the end of my barrel to be the size of a bullet. That signifies a near miss; well, after a hole was accidentally shot through my hand, and nearly killed me, I decided to not put any more holes in my hat. At one point in early 1997 after my hand was shot, over half my blood supply was gone. A 4 out of an 11 count.

The skies are pretty much overcast and it is cooler today. We go across the shady lane again, and then Glennis Young is called Front and Center by Officers Barry Woods and Mike Pendleton.

Glennis puts wet powder on his face as he is 'fresh fish'. He has had some trouble getting his Richmond rifle to go off. Skip has been helping him to 'keep his dress.' We march over a way at the Left Oblique. Today the Federal Cavalry come out to face us for a Special Ceremony to honor the memory of a high-ranking reenactor, important to this event, who died earlier this year. A rider-less horse is led between two lines of men with sabers drawn and arms at Present. Soon the battle will start, and our Wing Commander Barry Woods gets the Yankees mad, especially one officer. We won't back down and 'long story short' we hem in the Yanks. I fire 80 rounds at this event. We are marched back and I get lost leaving out as we cannot return the way we came in to the event.

This is July 12, 2014, and I attend a Memorial Service for Raymond 'Pete' Camper. It is being held today at Gethsemane Baptist Church, located off road 116 somewhere between Burnt Chimney and Roanoke, Va. Brother Judson just arrives, Skip Fletcher and Captain Mike Pendleton being already here. Ken and Susie Meador drive up beside me and I notice they bought their car at Dale Earnhardt Chevrolet in Newton, N.C. Earlier today I was in Newton as Lynell and I visited my oldest son and his family. We drove right past the dealership on our way to his house.

Around 40 people are inside the church for the service. Doug is a speaker; he and his dad were very close and reenacted together. I remember attending meetings with them at Salem, Va. of the Fincastle Rifles Sons of Confederate Veterans Camp #1326. They have been an inspiration and encouragement to me.

Afterwards, outside Confederate reenactors fire volleys. I give Doug Camper some pictures before I leave.

This is September 6, 2014, and I drive up to the other side of Westlake, Va., to the site of the Franklin County Civil War Days event. I arrive in the early dawn to get in a 'day' here.

I walk down to find Doug Camper and some 60th Va. boys. Skip Fletcher is making the rounds on a golf cart as the place slowly comes to life. Red Barbour, the Commander of the Fincastle Rifles S.C.V. camp #1326, helps bring in the breakfast from Bojangles. I get a meal ticket at registration along with Captain Pendleton and Robert Brown who also came in this morning. I shake hands with Bobby Compton and show him a magazine story on the 150th Gettysburg as he is mentioned in it. I buy some 'paper ladies' plus other items from the Sutlers. For 32 dollars, I get two pounds of black powder from Leon Craft. Red hands me another sausage biscuit before I head back to camp. As Captain Pendleton plays the fiddle, more folks arrive: Ken and Susie Meador, Terry and Joan Williams, Bremen Harrell, his sister Miss Lil, and Patrick Wells. Some Franklin County boys join us as they did last year.

Captain Pendleton talks to a new recruit. There are nineteen of us to go on the field where we join the 28th Va. led by Officer Lawhorn. In the battle, I take a 'hit' and at one point both sides are firing over me. After the battle, there is a Pass in Review. As I leave, a light rain starts and there is lightening in the distance.

This is September 12, 2014, and Lynell and I arrive at the Virginia Horse Center for the 150th Anniversary of Thunder in the Valley to find registration is closed for the day. We drive over to our camp site and Captain Pendleton directs us to our spot. Joan Williams helps us set up our tent on the end of the company street. Chuck Carter is here.

This is the morning of September 13, 2014, and we got some rain during the night. I cook sausage over a fire Leon Craft has made; Lynell has breakfast in bed. At the next camp, Bobby Compton works to start a fire. Slowly our camp comes to life. Terry, Richard (the new guy from last weekend), John, and Esther are in camp. Robert Brown drives up to report having seen heavy rain. We get accoutered up and the ten of us of the 51st go out for drill. We come back, post Colors, then go in the field where we are camping for Dress Parade, all under overcast skies. Artillery and dismounted Cavalry attend this parade. After Dress Parade, we have Battalion Drill where General Shelton gives Longstreet

Corps a pep talk and emphasizes attendance at Corps Events. After this, we have more Company Drill. At camp, we pick up Private Glennis Young, then we all have to go out for more Company Drill.

I hand out some ear plugs in camp then go buy a ten-pound bag of ice for three dollars. An Inspector comes around to inspect our camp and is escorted by 2nd Sgt. Brown. Capt. Pendleton comes back from the prebattle walk through and has us do a 'Guard against Cavalry' drill. Lynell and I eat some ham sandwiches before she goes out to find a hotel as she is feeling really bad. We get accoutered up to have a Weapons Inspection before marching up a big steep hill at a pace that is not leisurely. When we are finally halted, I nearly lose what little wind I have left from laughing upon hearing Chuck Carter say, "Where's the fire." After our 2 cannons on the hilltop fire, Capt. Pendleton leads us over the top to engage some far-off Yankee Cavalry. They come on up towards us shooting their pistols. Other of our troops join the fight. We fall back to form a battle line with the 1st Ky., then sweep forward. I take a 'hit' about halfway down the hill and save a considerable amount of ammo as the battle rages on for quite some time. I think this is the battle of Piedmont. Red Barbour is the announcer. The survivors of the battle 'Pass in Review' far below and out from where I am.

Some of us including some high-ranking officers walk back over the hill to camp. 2nd Sgt. Brown gets us all together to 'Break Ranks,' then we clean rifles. Allen Jackson and Jessica are breaking down their tent in preparation to leave. John and I are preparing more cartridges for a future battle. On the hill behind Capt. Pendleton sits Gen. Shelton with his two small children.

The sun is out now and I walk to the Sutlers with Richard and Chuck. I buy 'paper ladies' which is the name used for the already rolled paper tubes that we fill with black powder. It is preferred to fill them with 65 grains or so, then bend the top, and tuck this tail in the seam to make a cartridge. I also buy cleaning patches and another 'Gettysburg 135th Photographic Review'. I never checked in at the registration table at this event but I am sure we were paid up and preregistered. I talk with Daniel Young the blacksmith. Chuck and I get a ride most of the way back. Russell stops by for a chat. Chuck oversees John and Leon retiring Colors.

This is September 14, 2014, and Leon Craft has a good fire going which draws a crowd. At the next campfire over from ours lays Barry Wood and those that slept there on the ground last night. Kyle from South Boston, Va., who yesterday was training some 'new' guys, now converses with us. Officer Woods comes over to our fire to tell us a funny West Virginia story. 1st Sgt. Williams oversees the posting of our Colors, the Virginia State flag and our Battle flag. We are going about getting breakfast when Lynell comes in. We carry some things out to the pickup before she, still sick, leaves again for the hotel.

I have to go out to the Dress Parade. Officer Will Perkinson is the Parade Adjutant. Afterward, we have Battalion Drill, then at camp our company drills in stacking of arms. I take some pictures of Officer Bill Russell from the 150th Gettysburg over to his camp. Glennis and Margaret are back in camp and so is Ken and Susie. Ken displays another skill as he sews on the quilt helping the women.

This is the quilt to be raffled off. Joan is fixing Esther's hair under the tent fly which is a busy place. As I rest in the tent, I recall how last night I slept with my shirt, wool trousers, nine button shell jacket, socks, and brogans on. Lynell is back and is checked out of the hotel.

Soon, the soldiers are on the field for a Weapons Inspection. A new 1st Ky. Captain inspects my rifle before we are marched up the hill a different route. I look down the hill to see Lynell drives the truck in camp to load. Barry Woods is in charge of our right wing today. We wheel into position. There are some distant Yankee Cavalry on a distant hill, probably not more than a dozen Infantry soldiers spread out, and their Artillery being two cannons. The Confederate and Federal Cavalry clash sabers quite a bit today. Longstreet Corps has over a hundred rifles. We shift our position and also fire at the Right Oblique. On the hillside below one of our cannons, I happen to take a 'hit'. I had already burned through nearly a box of ammo. Richard lies just down the hill from me, his face with black powder on it signifying his new guy status and initiation into our company. This also helps in case he needs help quickly and the company knows to look out for him. At this time, I need help because one of our cannons is firing over my head.

This is the beginning of the end of my reenacting career. We Pass in Review. I will notice later that the ringing in my ears does not go away. Before the next event, I decide to make the 150th Anniversary Appomattox my last as a participant.

This is October 4, 2014, and on this Saturday morning, Lynell and I arrive at the J.E.B. Stuart Birthplace in Ararat, Virginia, to be here just for the day. Registration is not open. Leon Craft is rousing from his night's sleep in his van. Several soldiers are in camp.

Travis White, his two sons, and youngest daughter 'Boo Boo' are cooking and eating bacon. I shoulder a rifle on the Color Detail. We form up to march up the hill to have a Dress Parade with the galvanized Carolina Yankees. Next, we march over to the giant flagpole where Allen, Jessica, and Glennis get the big 2nd National Confederate flag flying. The man standing on one side of me at the ceremony is a Sharpshooter, meaning his rifle has a long scope on it. I go over to visit at the Wharton-Stuart Sons of Confederate Veterans Camp #1832 tent. At the Sutlers, I buy some Confederate money and then try to buy a $10.00 T-shirt with it. Lynell is here now, I get a crème soda refill and we sample food from the local vendors for lunch. I go down to register and get a 150th Anniversary yellow ribbon. In camp, I finish my distribution of pictures. Private Travis White playing his washboard is accompanying Captain Mike Pendleton whether he is playing his fiddle or his banjo.

Clad in their civilian attire are our visitors Lester Harrell and George Davis. 2nd Sgt. Brown sees that we are ready on time for the upcoming battle. The 51st Va. Infantry Company D fields 21 soldiers on this cool, sunny, breezy day. Going into the battle, we have already been scripted to lose. I fire all but two of my cartridges before taking a 'hit'. We Pass in Review.

This is October 17, 2014, and Lynell and I arrive across from the original Cedar Creek battlefield at registration just before 10 P.M. For this 150th Anniversary event, we receive nice medallions and wrist bands. We are preregistered so it shortens the process of checking in. We cannot use the parking lot near the Museum as in years past. We turn into a lot across from the corner store, and see Mike Broome and his wife who is also General Shelton's sister. We get a spot in back of a barn and sleep in back of the pickup truck.

This is October 18, 2014, and before 4:30 A.M. I am 'stirring about' and getting breakfast. I bid Lynell bye and start out walking to find the camp of the 51st Va. I probably walk a mile asking a few people in the darkness where Longstreet Corps is camped. I find them at the far end of the Confederate camp. I spot Pvt. Craft putting wood on a fire, next to it are Doug Camper and a couple of guys sleeping campaign style in their blankets. Leon lets me store things in his tent. The camps slowly come to life with the onset of daylight such as it is with

the skies being overcast. Ken and Susie are here with a framed picture of me taken at Trevilian Station. I am humbled by the kind gift. 1st Sgt. Williams and his wife Joan are here as is the 2nd Sgt. Brown.

Skip and Beverly Fletcher are in the tent beside of Leon's. John Alger, his daughter, and her friend are in camp, also Glennis and Margret Young. Allen Jackson has a little tent set up next to Captain Pendleton's tent. Various ones are getting breakfast.

Up the hill, I find Officer Barry Woods and give him a photo packet. Our 1st and 2nd sergeants flank Privates Leon and Richard in posting of Colors. Joe from the old 60th Va. is in our number of fourteen at Dress Parade. We are chosen to be Color Company. Colonel Bill Russell is our 2nd Battalion Commander. Richard goes to get our Battle Flag to give to the flag bearer Doug Camper. General Shelton comes down to preside over the Parade. The Bell Grove Plantation house is very prominent in the background of our Dress Parade.

The Parade seems unusually slow and is 'dragging' on when Doug starts to stagger. I put out my hand to catch him but he goes the other way and then on to the ground. Some Medics rush in. The Parade starts back up and afterwards Doug is escorted back to camp. Company Drill is led by Captain Pendleton, then Battalion Drill is led by Colonel Bill Russell. Afterwards, we have more Company Drill.

Back at camp, we Stack Arms.

I take a packet of 150th Gettysburg photos to Adcock who I don't remember seeing since Gettysburg. I give out more pictures. Capt. Pendleton, 1st Sgt. Williams, and I head for the Sutlers. Upon arrival, we part ways. I have my camcorder and film some Federals having a big review.

I can see many of the 5,000 reenactors at this event are wearing blue. Above the Sutlers, the 2nd South Carolina String Band is playing and then up walks Bobby Compton in a top hat to join them in a number by playing the 'bone's'. I put in my 'music' camera chip that has Travis and Mike playing music on it, but the camera must be out of 'juice.' I now regret the filming wasted on the Yankees. I go over to the pickup to have lunch with Lynell before hurrying back to camp.

We are confined to camp before we accouter up and march up to the dirt road above camp for a Weapons Inspection. Now the Corps will begin its slow march to the battlefield. Private Fletcher reads from the Good Book and Private Jackson leads us in prayer.

Colonel Russell marches us forward then By the Right Flank. We are marched about a bit then finally get to shooting and advancing. The Heater House is off to our right front. No one is 'affected' by the enemy gunfire for a while. We cross a ravine and are heading up a rocky slope when Skip Fletcher takes a terrible 'hit.' He is howling in great pain when the captain tries to talk him out of it. Allen Jackson goes over with his rifle butt to 'put him out of his misery'. Sarcastically, I tell Allen he would make a great nurse. Soon, John Alger is down. At the furthest line of our advance, I take a 'hit' after having fired 42 times.

Soon the Yanks come sweeping down. I take pictures and look over a ways to see Henry Kidd down also taking pictures.

The battle ends with the Confederates back about where they started and one of my pictures is of a Billy Yank and a Johnny Reb shaking hands.

Leon said he ran out of ammo about three shots from the end, and Allen ran out of caps. Doug Camper carried the Confederate Battle Flag throughout the battle. We get marched back to the road above camp and hear good remarks from General Shelton concerning our role in the battle. I get my few things and return to the pickup where Lynell takes pictures of me with my rifle.

We eat supper and sleep in the truck. At 5 A.M., we start for home.

CHAPTER 10 - 2015

This is January 17, 2015, and time for the 150ᵗʰ Anniversary Battle of Ft. Fisher located on the coast of North Carolina at the mouth of the Cape Fear River.

Lynell and I stayed last night in Carolina Beach. We drive the road leading to Ft. Fisher and pass various law enforcement vehicles and the Museum. I have to park on down near the ocean off of the paved road. I walk back up to the Museum and, at the front desk, show a young lady the things I have brought for the idea of displaying.

I want to get the exactly 150-year-old letter I have for display in the Museum. It was penned near here by my captured great-great grandfather Samuel A. Dowless to his wife Sarah.

I also have the copy of a picture of Samuel and his brother Elisha, who was also in the battle; something I wrote exactly twenty years ago when I reenacted here; something I wrote when I was at Point Lookout, Maryland where the brothers were imprisoned; and other pictures and papers concerning the situation. Now an elderly man working here helps to explain the materials would have been needed to have been submitted earlier. I start showing people on my own. Outside I go to two Sons of Confederate Veterans tents that are set up and a 'Friends of Ft. Fisher' tent and share my story. There is a tent nearby with displays on marines, as both C.S. and U.S. Marines fought at this place.

Some of these reenactors cross the road to Ft. Fisher's Battle Acre where the U.S. Marine Corps Band is on site with many other people. The Governor of North Carolina with his team walks by and soon addresses the crowd.

I am pleased that the U.S. Marine Corps Band plays 'Dixie' as one of their selections.

I meet up with Lynell; the day has not gone as planned. We were just going to stop by so I could go in the Museum and see about displaying the items or at least some of them. Then, we were planning to return to the hotel room where I would write up captions for the display and change into my Confederate uniform. Now it is so crowded, plus the letter did not make it, and I am dejected.

I walk over to the nearby Atlantic Ocean where Yankee ships had blasted the earthen fort for three days before a combined U.S. sailor and marine attack was repulsed by the fort's defenders. The land-based attack by their army succeeded after bloody hand-to-hand combat and, arguably, the best General the North had, Southerner Braxton Bragg, held back Confederate soldiers he could have sent to reinforce the fort's defenders. Ft. Fisher had protected blockade runners for years as they brought in supplies from England.

I walk up and through the Confederate camp to the spectator rope and continue telling my ancestor's story and my own of reenacting. This is my first event as a spectator since I began reenacting in 1993. This is an invitation only event, no walk-ons permitted, so they say. Twenty years ago, my brother Jud and I did walk-on. That time, the fighting was at night with fireworks helping to simulate battle, now cannon fire opens the battle in bright cold sunshine.

The Yankees eventually make it over the large earthen humps, and come in by the river 'pushing' the Confederates back toward us.

All the reenactors did a good job of freezing this moment in time for me, and all too soon the bugle sounds. I utilized my spectator status to film and photograph. I go through Sutler Row and back into the Museum. In the Registry Book, I give my name, address, and in the comments section I write the following: To- Samuel Dowless, I was here. These are the words from his letter:

Near Fort Fisher, N. C. January the seventeen-day 1865

Mrs. Sarah J. Dowless

Dear wife and children

I drop a line to let you no that I am well and harty and all so in the hands of the Yankees and they treat me very kind. I hope this may find you all well and enjoying the blessings of God. My Dear I don't no where tha will carry me to don't be unesay about me. God is with me pray put your trust in God. I will rite to you every chance. Brother Elisha is wounded but is about well and if this is our parting letter By the Grace of God I will meat you in heaven. I ever remain your true and affectionnate husban until death. S.A. Dowless to Sarah J. Dowless

They had seven children before he volunteered for service in the Confederacy and served in the 36th N. C. Heavy Artillery 2nd Co. I. He was captured and imprisoned. After the war he returned home to Bladen County where they were blessed with six more children. The last child being my great-grandfather.

This is February 7, 2015, and time for the annual Meeting of the 51st Va. Inf. Co. D. Around five miles or so from our house, the meeting is held in Woolwine Va. at the Smith River Rescue Squad Building. Lynell's contribution to the feast that follows Allen Jackson's prayer is listed here; Turkey, dressing, potatoes, broccoli casserole, relish tray, rolls, pecan pies, and a large soda to drink. I have video camera, pictures, and the 150's journal. Around 27 people are in attendance. I hand out pictures. Mike Pendleton goes back in as Captain as does Terry Williams as 1st Sgt. Waynesboro, Bentonville, and Appomattox are all that's on my schedule of events as I will not be reenacting after the last 150th event on our roster. For the first time they vote to go to Ft. Branch. I pay $25.00 for our dues. I find out Ken Meador went to Ft. Fisher and I find him in some of my camera photo's that I draw up closer. Ken sets up his tripod for a group photo of us all.

This is March 20, 2015, and I arrive, finally, at the site of the 150th Anniversary Battle of Bentonville, North Carolina. At the Registration Tent, they want my last name, then first name, as they check on laptop computers. The lady says I will have to pay seven dollars above the preregistration to get the Event Medallion, which I promptly do. I get paper parking and event passes. It's a huge parking lot and a nice black gentleman shows me where to park. I walk dressed as I went to work today and it is easy to get through the Yankee camp. I see in the darkness a Yankee take several steps backward, before he hits the ground, drunk. I cross on a wooded trail over to the Confederate camp. Longstreet Corps tents are the first Confederate tents I see; I know this because I recognize the silhouette of Mike Broome of the First Kentucky. I am unable to locate any of the 51st Va. An Officer's Meeting is going on nearby in the dim light. I walk up to Sutler row and get a candle. Over at the 'Fall Creek Sutlery,' I get the 2nd South Carolina String Band CD called 'Strike the Tent', and a book entitled Black Southerners in Confederate Armies. I go back to the pickup camper shell where I plan to spend the night.

This is March 21, 2015, and I slept well last night. I get dressed to head out wearing black wool trousers, brogans, the butternut block-I buttoned sack coat, and butternut kepi. I hear the Yankee bands playing wake up songs as I walk over to Longstreet Corps Headquarters and hear General Shelton snoring. I am looking for the camp of the 51st when I hear my name called by Captain Pendleton. I put my rifle and accoutrements on my gum blanket under the captain's tent fly, in case it rains. The captain as well as some others slept in vehicles last night. I get some beef jerky to eat then Skip Fletcher gives me some hardtack. Ken Meador surprises me with the gift of a tripod! He and Joe have their tents set up, Skip's is near the fire where Doug Camper and two young soldiers are campaigning. Travis White, Hannah, and Destiny are here with a tent.

Isaac White stays in a nice lean-to shelter. The memory of five years ago is still fresh in the minds of some of us; when in the deep woods, we lugged in and out so much stuff. This time, the camp is nearer the field. The day is warming up, complete with sunshine.

Morning Colors are posted. We go out minus haversacks to Dress Parade which is on the big field behind the Sutlers. Plenty of other Confederate units are out here drilling and doing Dress Parades of their own. We are Color Company in Officer Bill Russell's 1st Battalion of Longstreet Corps. I line up right behind the

flag bearer. Ken and Skip flank him as they are guards on the detail. Officer Kyle is the Adjutant and General Shelton presides.

Another Command Unit is having a Dress Parade with a band for their music, we have no music. We go into Company and Battalion Drill.

Back at our camp, Leon and I strike out for the parking lot, taking the route through the Yankee camp area. I pick up some pictures to hand out. We see Glennis Young, they have a really nice pickup. We stop at the food vendors. Here is one of the biggest Sutler Rows one can see in reenacting. Leon and I get Bentonville 150th programs for $5.00 each. Kids are enjoying playing about a lone brass cannon in the earth works at the entrance to our camps.

I give 8X10's to Travis White and pictures to Ken Meador of him at Ft. Fisher. Captain Mike Pendleton gets out his fiddle and Private Travis White his washboard to make music for our ears. About 5 minutes before we are to get accoutered up, in walks 1st Sgt. Terry Williams and his wife Joan. She will be visiting a sister who lives nearby.

We form up on the dirt road and get inspected, now I am behind Ken. We march through the woods and the Yankee camp on our way to stage in the woods off the battlefield near the parking lot. Pictured below is the 28th Virginia.

We come out of the woods on the attack firing and advancing. One time, I am put on Color guard a short time due to the detail's 'hits'. Back in the fray, I have shot about 50 times and then go down at the furthest of our advance. Our guys are falling back. Some Yanks get in a trench line. Soon some Confederates advance on line. I have moved closer to Isaac White and get him to help me in filming over my shoulder.

I am laying at Joe Owen's foot and we get a lot of sand on us from what used to be a corn field. Above us, Confederates hit their line in a charge; below us, the Yanks come over the earth works. The battle rages on a good while before it ends. What is left of the 51st Va. is in the tree line again.

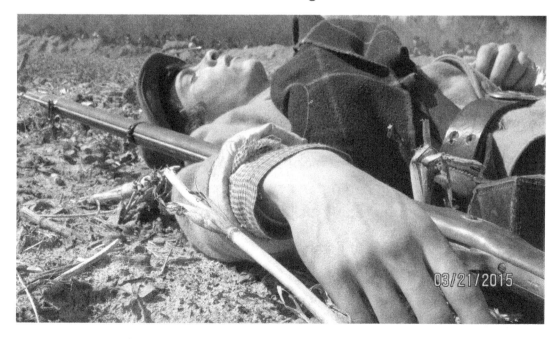

We reform and march by cheering spectators on our way back to camp where, with the use of the new tripod, get a company photo.

We set in on some rifle cleaning. Joe Owen and Ken Meador go to get some food. The Capt., 1st Sgt., Skip, and I go looking for something to drink. Some Yanks guarding Confederate prisoners are all posing for a camera of the times. I take advantage of the set up to get my own photo. I get some water and we all set at a table, many folks are about. We go back to camp, and the food I had Ken to get is here as we had put in orders. I have seafood and lots of it before heading back to the pickup truck for the night.

This is March 22, 2015, and I had only one nightmare due to going to bed with a full stomach. I leave out walking, carrying only my rifle and accouterments and soon see Glennis Young as we head for camp. I count 108 Port-o-Johns before we get there. Leon Craft comes on later to join those of us around the fire. Colors are posted near the large pine tree as it was yesterday.

We get ready, form up on the road, and march out to the big field beside the Sutlers for our music-less Dress Parade. We don't do all the drill as we did yesterday. I give Glennis my rifle to take back to camp so I can get the cartridge tubes I should have gotten yesterday. I walk these to the pickup where I switch out the kepi for my black weathered slouch hat, still turned up in front but minus the Virginia State Seal metal pin. As I enter our camps, General Shelton and I exchange salutes; he has his two small children with him. I sit on the wood pile as Joe Owen tells me about the battle of New Market Heights.

Robert Brown is with us now; he came in during Dress Parade. He got to visit the Sutlers with Terry and Conner.

Now, as we sit around the fire, we are caught off guard when we see others getting ready. We expected the First Call to come later. Now we scramble to get out to the road.

Longstreet Corps is marched out to the Parade field, past other of our troops, down past the Historical house, a left turn through woods, into a field with lots of spectators, past our cannon crews, and into a long field to wait behind some trees. We Stack Arms and rest nearby. I watch as Russell draws a picture of Nathan as we are passing the time.

We get called to Take Arms then shoot through about 30 yards of trees at some Yanks on the edge of a large field. We charge through the trees to give chase a way as we fire and advance. We are still Color Company and Ken and Skip are still guards, but today non- combatant Richard carries a 1st National flag of sorts in this late war battle. We are commanded to Right Face and run for the tree line. I see this confusion as a time to sneak out my camcorder to film. I have turned while on the run in this plowed up cotton field and step off into an abandoned Yankee fox hole, with the camera still running. Two guys offer assistance as I scramble up, only my pride hurt. On the film, it really looks like I was shot. We wait in the trees and listen to the sounds of battle. We hear the distant sound of the Henry repeating rifles, a late war rifle. We come out and begin advancing into the enemy's fire, Officer Bill Russell leading the way. At what will be our farthest advance Capt. Pendleton says, "start taking some 'hits'."

I get down and he says, "Mark get your camera and take pictures" or something to that effect.

Our men fall back then the Yankees come up to about ten yards from me to form their new battle line. Needless to say, I get some great pictures and video from between the two lines.

Once, a smiling Yank looked at me because he knew I was getting great 'film footage'. They fall back as the battle slows down.

I limp back to our boys and make sure I thank Captain Mike Pendleton. The Confederate Command Structure for the 150th Anniversary Battle of Bentonville, N.C. is as follows: Commanding General Major General Jake Jennette; 1st Division, Bvt. General Bill Potts Commanding 1st Division, Army of Northern Virginia and Provisional Army of the Confederate States; 2nd Division, Major General Terry Shelton, Commanding Longstreet Corps and FFR; 3rd Division, Bvt. Brig. General Chris Roberts, Commanding Carolina Legion, Southern Division, Dept. of the Gulf, French Broad and Claiborne; Artillery, Colonel Randy Hines, Chief of Artillery; Cavalry Bvt. General Doug Nalls, Commanding.

This is April 10, 2015, and after putting in our day's work and traveling some more, we are at Appomattox, Virginia, at dark. We pull in at the NPS and ask a man who just drove down from the State of Maine for directions. A Park Service Officer comes to my window, his dad is from Maine. Soon, they are talking to each other as we sit between them. I drive over, park, then walk, and ran on gravel roads in the dark to find a Confederate camp. I am told this is just one of the reenactment sites. I view Historic buildings and go back for my camera. I get a picture of the restored McClean House as the camera flash goes off.

04/10/2015

We leave and are soon lost. We drive in back of the closed Museum of the Confederacy. In town, I stop for directions and buy a paper with news of the event. We turn in at the Industrial Park, and wonder why we could not have had our reenactment at the Appomattox Court House?

We find Chuck Carter and his wife at the registration table, and we get wooden circles that double for passes and souvenirs. We start down the hill, then decide to turn around at the Sutlers. The ground is feeling slippery. We cross the muddy road to the muddy parking lot and get stuck here. The place had been hammered by a storm before we got here. A guy hooks a chain to my bumper and a tractor pulls me to some gravel. We are very fortunate and, in answer to Lynell's prayer, get a spot near the road we crossed earlier. We set about getting into the back of the truck under the camper shell and get the area ready for the night. I take the lantern and packets of pictures with me in search of the camp of the 51st Va. I give one pack to Officer Kyle, don't know his last name. I then take another one to the captain of the 28th Va. and one to the captain of the 1st Ky. He directs me to where the camp of the 51st Va. is located. I had been by here earlier but of course did not recognize the two soldiers from Poland at the camp. Now, I talk to one and give him picture packets to put in his tent for me to hand out tomorrow. Going up the hill, I help push out a stuck truck. I see now Sutler 'Old Doc Bell' is closing up.

This is April 11, 2015, and Lynell and I slept well. I get up to get ready while there is still a half moon in the sky. I eat a little something at the truck. I leave with my rifle, accouterments, and an 8X10 from Cedar Creek. Lynell is going as far as the Port-o-Johns, and we get stopped by Robert Brown who has just arrived and asks directions. Lynell will never make it down to the camp today. She tells me later that she slipped twice before going back to the truck. I go on down to camp and see Travis White is here with his girls. Jessica is also here. I hear she is soon to be married to Allen Jackson. Robert comes in and I help post Colors as a guard.

The company has just gone out on a tactical. I hand a photo in an envelope to an officer. The company on the next street goes out, it is the 1st Texas under Capt. Tim Smith. Later, the men return from a tactical that the Yankees did not show up to. One of the three men from Poland, that will fall in with our company at this event, retrieves the pictures he kept in his tent for me, and I proceed to hand them out. We help John Alger set up his tents and later push his vehicle out of the mud.

Above are the 3 men from Poland who joined us for this event.

Captain Pendleton calls for a formation. Present are Robert, John, Terry, Ken, Travis, Allen, Jessica, Skip, Glennis, Doug, Desmond, Richard, Isaac, Leon, a man from Oklahoma, and the three men from Poland. The captain calls me Front and Center.

On one end of the street, I remember two women, Joan and Beverly, taking pictures. Captain Pendleton presents me with a nice plaque and a 'Cracker Barrell' gift card for Lynell. I salute then wave my weathered slouch hat in return to their three cheers to me. The plaque has a Virginia State Seal at the top and reads as follows:

In Recognition of Mark Leviner For his Defense of the Southern States

On and Off the Battlefield and for his Service to the 51st Va. Vol. Inf. Co. D.

'Deo Vindice'

Given on this Day 11 April 2015

Here at Appomattox, Va.

This is my last event as a participant and the first for Desmond Fifer. I take the gestures of love and kindness in the form of these gifts up to the truck. Lynell is still unable to change into the period attire due to all the people passing by. On my way back down the hill, I spot Al Stone portraying General Lee riding on Traveler. His staff ride with him.

I get pictures and I will get quite a few today. Further on, I pass a pile of limbs and a mannequin stretched out on a cot. Chuck Carter is on the Event Staff and rides by on a 4-wheeler pulling a wagon. 2nd Sgt. Brown has some of us go out to help the new guy, Desmond Fifer, with learning drill. We have twenty soldiers in our company photo. George and Sam Davis are some of those visiting us in street clothes. Soon we go out to one of the largest Dress Parades I've ever been in. Afterwards, we hear the Yankees are brewing for a fight.

We get to go in camp for our haversacks then return to the ranks. A Weapons Inspection now follows. I get inspected by the lady Sergeant O' Driscoll. We march out to the battlefield and soon become hotly engaged.

Colonel Barry Woods is in charge of us and, as usual, we make the Yankees mad. We flank a bunch of them, then end up behind them with more of our troops in front of them. I don't take a hit and I fire many a shot. Marching back, I am behind one of the Polish soldiers.

We clean rifles in camp. I will not even take out my ear plugs until after the next battle. Some of the Company have been here a few days and have horror stories to tell of the mud. The fellows tell me yesterday they had to remove their vehicles far from camp, but then on walking back, were told they didn't have to. Now there are many other peoples' vehicles around in the camps. The rain changed the way some things were done in camp at this event. The wind that is now drying things out also blows our Virginia State Seal and Confederate Battle flags I helped post earlier.

I hang out around camp and watch a horse drawn wagon out in a field away from the muddy road. We form up again and I get inspected by the same Sergeant as before. As we are marching out to the battlefield, I am asked by Allen Jackson has it hit me yet, to which I reply, "I just want the battle to start and fight the battle," or something to that effect. Before this battle, we wait and get to see 'General Lee' ride by. The cannons duel for quite some time. I tell the boys we have to win this one for I fear what will happen in 150 years from now. This must have had an effect for in this big battle, not one of the 51st Va. is 'killed' or 'wounded'.

We Clear Weapons and march back, I having already fired my last shot in a reenactment; tomorrow the surrender is slated. This is my first time doing an

Appomattox reenactment and my last event, all in one. We stand at attention in the ranks and on being dismissed, shout, 'VIRGINIA'. I am the only one who steps back, turns right and starts walking up the hill. Nearing the top, my attention is drawn to the music of the 2nd South Carolina String Band who are set up across the muddy road from the Sutlers.

They just seem to know that I, in my ragged clothes, have been doing this a while and seeing my rifle on my shoulder, sense I have fought my last battle. They start playing the music to the 'Ashokan Farewell' and I feel something start to happen inside of me. I sit down and start to record on the video camera. I cannot stop the camera; I only wish I had a hundred-dollar bill to hand each one of these men. At a tent, I get two bags of information made up for reenactors as Lynell and I were preregistered. When I approach the pickup, I see my wife Lynell sitting in the wooden straight back chair we brought, in her 1860's clothing. She smiles at me and I can hold back the tears no longer.

We take a few pictures and she puts one on 'Facebook' with info that this is our last event. It is at this point, that we decide to leave out and not stay here for the Surrender Ceremony tomorrow. It has now hit me and I probably would not be much good around the fellas anyway. Today sadness has found me.

We now find the 2000 S10 pickup is stuck in 4-wheel drive. Something must have broken last night in our attempts to get unstuck. The indicator light is out. We can hardly go 35 mph. and police cars seem to be everywhere with their lights flashing. We pull off at two places and I still cannot get the thing to go in 2 high. I get Lynell to praying. We pull in at an 'Advance Auto' store and for thirty some dollars we have a new part in and the light works on 2 high now! Thank God!

We drive over to the real Appomattox Village and the NPS informs us we will have to go about two miles down the road to park. WE can then ride back on a shuttle bus in order to just cross the parking lot here that I had parked in last night.

We follow the instructions while we remain dressed in our period attire. The sun is setting now on us and our time as reenactors. We enjoy walking in the late evening sun in the village. In the bookstore, one of the best on this time in history that there is, I buy a magnet of the Mclean House for Lynell. We stand at the top of the steps of this famous house that has been rebuilt to match its original stateliness.

Here we do our last deed as reenactors as we remember 150 years ago on April 9th the Generals, Lee and Grant. We are saddened by the surrender of General Lee and his Army, but realize America as one nation will be stronger when it has to deal with other Nations of the world. At what seems to be an impossibility, we find a Motel room in Appomattox to spend the night as someone had canceled their reservations. As a 'career' recap, I was a Confederate reenactor from the age of 34 until the age of 56, and all was done from the rank of a Private, this meant I got to do a lot of shooting. I participated in 132 events and attended an extra one as a spectator. As a participant, I aimed and 'shot' at Yankees in every event except the 145th Gettysburg where I was on General Shelton's Staff. Some have reenacted for shorter, and some have reenacted for longer periods of time than me. This is only one person's story; each reenactor has their own. Every mile I traveled, all the money I invested, and all the time spent reenacting is just a small tribute to the Trinity believing Confederate soldiers I represented, and what they endured for the love of their God, families, fellow soldiers, and the Southland.

I found this Confederate doubled barreled cannon in Athens, Georgia thanks to my oldest son John.

AFTERWORD

They say the winners get to write the history books. The South lost the war, but they won my heart and I am writing this book. Having said this, I'm sure you have heard the winner's side of this chapter in American history. When it comes to the causes of the war being fought, let's hear from some who fought it and from some who lived in that time. The following quotes are taken from a list of 54 found in "The War for Southern Independence or Slavery?" Read the truthful statements from our History:

"Every man should endeavor to understand the meaning of subjugation before it is too late...it means the history of this heroic struggle will be written by the enemy; that our youth will be trained by Northern schoolteachers; will learn from Northern school books their version of the war, will be impressed by the influences of history and education to regard our gallant dead as traitors, and our maimed veterans as fit objects for derision...It is said slavery is all we are fighting for, and if we give it up we give up all. Even if this were true, which we deny, slavery is not all our enemies are fighting for. It is merely a pretense to establish sectional superiority and a more centralized form of government, and to deprive us of our rights and liberties." -Maj. General Patrick R. Cleburne, CSA, January 1864, writing on what would happen if the Confederacy were to be defeated.

"'My paramount object in this struggle is to save the Union, and it is not either to save or destroy slavery. If I could save the Union without freeing any slave I would do it, and if I could save it by freeing all the slaves I would do it; and if I could save it by freeing some and leaving others alone, I would also do that." - Abraham Lincoln, 22 August 1862, in a letter to Horace Greeley, editor of the New York Tribune.

'If it [the Declaration of Independence] justifies the secession from the British empire of 3,000,000 of colonists in 1776, we do not see why it would not justify the secession of 5,000,000 of Southrons from the Federal Union in 1861. If

Page | 299

we are not mistaken on this point, why does not some one attempt to show wherein why?" -New York Tribune, 17 December 1860.

"The sole object of this war is to restore the Union. Should I become convinced it has any other object, or that the Government designs its soldiers to execute the wishes of the Abolitionists, I pledge you my honor as a man and a soldier I would resign my commission and carry my sword to the other side." -General Ulysses S. Grant, USA, in a letter to the Chicago Tribune, 1862.

'So far from engaging in a war to perpetuate slavery, I am rejoiced that slavery is abolished." -General Robert E. Lee CSA.

"There are few, I believe, in this enlightened era who would not agree with me that slavery as an institution is a moral and political evil." – General Robert E. Lee CSA.

"I wish to see the shackles struck from every slave." -Lt. General Thomas J. 'Stonewall' Jackson, CSA.

"The Northern onslaught upon slavery is no more than a specious humbug designed to conceal its desire for economic control of the Southern States." -Charles Dickens, 1862.

I would be amiss if I didn't give a little more insight on Abraham Lincoln at this juncture.

"In saving the Union I have destroyed the Republic." -Abraham Lincoln.

"[Lincoln] was an infidel of the radical type... never mentioned the name of Jesus, except to scorn and detest the idea of a miraculous conception." -William Hemdon, law partner to Abraham Lincoln.

"The Emancipation Proclamation...professes to emancipate all slaves in places where the United States authorities cannot exercise any jurisdiction...but it does not decree emancipation...in any states occupied by federal troops." -Earl Russell, Britain's Foreign Secretary.

"I am not in favor of making voters or jurors of Negroes, nor of qualifying them to hold office...I am not in favor of Negro citizenship." -Abraham Lincoln.

"I will say, then, that I am not, nor have ever been in favor of bringing about in any way the social and political equality of the white and black races...I am in favor of having the superior position assigned to the white race." -Abraham Lincoln.

"Amend the Constitution to say it should never be altered to interfere with slavery." -Abraham Lincoln, 24 December 1860, presenting his stand on slavery to the Senate.

Here are just some of the ways that Abraham Lincoln violated the Constitution as can be found in the booklet, "Honest Abe Wasn't Honest":

He suspended the Writ of Habeas Corpus, Article 1, Section 9, Clause 2.

He declared war without the consent of Congress in 1861, which is a violation of Article 1 Section 8, Clause 11 and 12.

The Emancipation Proclamation, which is a violation of Article 4, Section 3, Clause 2.

He made West Virginia a State in violation of Article 4, Section 3, Clause 1. He just separated Virginia and made West Virginia a State all by himself.

The Liberty of the Press was taken away-that a violation of the first Amendment.

Various people were involved in the capture of, the importation of, the selling of, the employment of, and the use of slaves. In a newsletter of the Craig Mountain Boys 28th Va., I find that from the slave coast, millions were sold into slavery by African Kings such as Ashanti, Dahomey, Adra, and Gelele. I have ancestry from the West Coast of Africa and the Congo so it is a possibility here of me being kin to the kings as well as the slaves. In the book Facts the Historians Leave Out, I find British and Dutch vessels transported slaves, as well as American ships; practically every one of them owned and operated by a Northerner. The Puritans of Massachusetts would capture and sell to the West Indies their Pequat Indian neighbors. They imported black slaves, at least 23,000 recorded, between 1775 and 1776. In 1778, the state of Rhode Island was first in the trafficking of slaves and later the state of New York took over the top spot. After the year 1808, it was unlawful to import slaves, but the trafficking continued; in 1820, Congress branded the slave trade as piracy. The traders defied the law for money. In 1860, the South had some 3,500,000 slaves for whom millions of dollars had been paid to the Northern traders.

To look at early slavery in America, I draw your attention to this from- Virginia, Guide to The Old Dominion, WPA Writers' Program, Oxford University Press, NY. 1940, p. 378., it states:

"In 1650, there were only 300 negroes in Virginia, about one percent of the population. They weren't slaves any more than the approximately 4,000 white indentured servants working out their loans for passage money to Virginia, and who were granted 50 acres each when freed from their indentures, so they could raise their own tobacco.

Slavery was established in 1654 when Anthony Johnson, Northampton County, convinced the court that he was entitled to the lifetime services of John Casor, a negro. This was the first judicial approval of life servitude, except as punishment for a crime.

But who was Anthony Johnson, winner of this epoch-making decision? Anthony Johnson was a negro himself, one of the original 20 brought to Jamestown {1619} and 'sold' to the colonists. By 1623 he had earned his freedom and by 1651 was prosperous enough to import five 'servants' of his own, for which he received a grant of 250 acres as 'headrights'.

Anthony Johnson ought to be in a 'Book of Firsts'. As the most ambitious of the first 20, he could have been the first negro to set foot on Virginia soil. He was Virginia's first free negro and first to establish a negro community, first negro landowner, first negro slave owner and as the first, white or black, to secure slave status for a servant. He was actually the founder of slavery in Virginia."

According to the 1830 National Census, 3,775 black slaveowners possessed altogether 12, 760 slaves. Free black women as well as free black men owned black slaves. The city of Charleston, South Carolina was a place where this was very prevalent.

Charleston, South Carolina, had a large Jewish population, and many were Confederate soldiers. General Grant, USA, had all Jews expelled from his department. On the other hand, there was in the Confederate Cabinet the Jew Judah Benjamin, born in the West Indies and raised in Charleston, S.C. He served as the Confederate Attorney General, Secretary of War, and Secretary of State. He was known as 'The Brains of the Confederacy'.

Many who say the war was over slavery may not know that in the time of 1828-1832, a war almost broke out, and it concerned tariffs. South Carolina had passed nullification laws because the U.S. Congress had increased the tariff rate on imported goods to 40 percent. During Reconstruction 1865-1877, the North got what it really wanted, resources of the South for pennies on the dollar. Abraham Lincoln promised the Northern Industrialists that he would increase tariffs if elected. He increased the tariff on iron to 50 and 51 percent.

The United States was founded as a Constitutional Federal Republic with limited Federal Government and sovereign States. The Confederate soldiers fought for the type of Government paid for in blood by their forebears in the American Revolution. Abraham Lincoln and the North fought against this to change America from a Constitutional Federal Republic to a Democracy with Socialist leanings. Socialist Karl Marx sent Abraham Lincoln, after his reelection in 1864, a letter of congratulations. Thomas Jefferson said, 'The best Government is that which governs least'.

When I first look into dads side of the family, it is shrouded in mystery. One thing is certain, according to my DNA, he had an ancestor who goes back into the Bourbon Kings of France, as one day King Louis XVI could say. Symon Lovina was born before 1660 and married a slave woman named Jean Tucker. Her father being Chief Peter the Great Nansmond Tucker, her master Major John Nichols, and her children John and Sarah born 1680 and 1682. John Nichols claims his slave woman Jean is a negro, but I read her father is an Indian. Jeans children in John Nichols 11 November1696 Norfolk Co. Will [WB6, fol. 950-96] receive their freedom plus land. Sarah gets 200 acres and John 150 and a160 acre tract also. These lands laid on the banks of the Western and Southern Branches of the Elizabeth River in Norfolk Co. Virginia. In a 1704 Quit Roll Leviner is being used. William Leviner moves into Bertie Co. North Carolina then John is living in Richmond Co. N.C. where generations later my dad Terry Edison Leviner is born in 1929. Some of the Leviners who served in the Confederacy are Enoch J. Ga. 2nd Cav. Co. A, Hyram S.C. 26th Inf. Co. D, Isaac Va. Lt. Arty. 12 Bn. Co. D, and J.M. S.C. 26th Inf. Co. D, he is the only Leviner on the Appomattox paroles. Great Great Uncle Perry Levina S.C. 1st [Butler's] Inf. Co. E was killed inside of Ft. Moultrie, South Carolina.

The Seal of the Confederacy has an equestrian stature of George Washington surrounded by the major crops of the South.

Thomas Hester of Bladen County, North Carolina, was born on April 2, 1757, and would serve in the Militia at various times and went to various places for a combined total of nine months of service. Once, he was surprised by the British at Brier Creek which he swam across to escape. Another time, he was in the repulse of the Tories at Ashpole Bear Swamp. The Patriots listed here are all from my mom's side of the family.

Another ancestor, who served in the American Revolution, is Private William Allen 1749-1831. He served in the 10th N.C. Regiment and was in the battle of Moore's Creek Bridge. He was married to Martha Shuffel and of their seven sons three served in the War of 1812. One of these being a fourth great grandfather of mine, Joseph Allen.

Ancestor Jacob Ballard Boyt was born April 4, 1755 out of wedlock and after his father John Ballard married someone else, he was raised by his grandfather Thomas Boyte; he used the last name Boyte/Boyt. He served in the N.C. Militia Continental Line, first in the Dobbs County Militia which became Wayne County. He was at the battle of Brier Creek, if you will, on the other side of the river guarding the baggage. It's possible he saw Thomas Hester.

Yet another ancestor on my mother's side of the family, who fought in the American Revolution, is James Cain 1748-1826 from South Carolina but whose family roots are found in Ireland. He was one of four patriots wounded in the battle of Elizabethtown, N.C. Here, 69 patriots out-smarted and defeated over 300 Tories, killing seventeen in the process. A descendant of his was Private Samuel A. Dowless, CSA., in next picture on the right. His brother Elisha on the left also a Private. Both of the men were married and each had 13 children. The 13th child of Samuel's being my great-Grandfather.

None of us had anything to do with our ancestry, no choice to whom we would be born to, nothing to do with when or where either. We can, however, if we wish to, look with compassion and respect upon everyone, because God made us all for His glory.

Half of my DNA is from the United Kingdom and Ireland. The places with the strongest evidences of my DNA in the UK are found in 1. Greater London, 2. Merseyside, 3. Glasgow City, 4. Greater Manchester, 5. West Midlands, 6. Tyne and Wear, 7. Lancashire, 8. South Yorkshire, 9. Belfast, and 10. City of Bristol.

In Ireland, the ten counties with the strongest evidence of my DNA are Dublin, Galway, Mayo, Kerry, Limerick, Cork, Kilkenny Cavan, Clare, and Donegal.

French and German show up at 11.4%, Scandinavian 3.3%, Spanish and Portuguese 1.3%, Finnish 1.2%; these making up part of the 91% of my European background.

From the 6.5% of my African ancestry, evidence of my ancestry can be found in the Countries of Nigeria, Ghana, Liberia, Sierra Leone, Angola, Congo, Senegal, and Guinea. I have 1.3% of Native American and some South Asian which can be found in the Countries of India, Pakistan, Afghanistan, and Bangladesh. I believe the 0.6% unassigned is European Jew because I have an aunt that has 2% of it. She is Dian May, my mother's sister who had her DNA tested and they are 100% European.

The point of this is my DNA is Confederate, altogether it made me the Confederate reenactor I was.

These lines are dedicated to; the memory of those Confederates who put their bodies in harm's way on behalf of their belief in God, their families, their fore bearers, and their South which exercised its Constitutional right to secede, to the Confederate soldier who stood in the ranks having lost both of his arms in combat, who replied when asked by the inspecting Officer what can you do?, 'I can yell sir', and to also include such men as some would not want to recognize in history as an example is here of black Confederate soldiers, these fought in the same regiment as my great-great Grandfather and both being in the 36th N.C. Heavy Artillery. Charles and Henry Dempsey, Privates, Company F, 36 N.C. Regiment (2 N.C. Artillery), Negros. Captured at Ft. Fisher January 15, 1865 and confined at Point Lookout MD. Until paroled and exchanged at Coxes Landing, James River, Va. February 14-15, 1865.

I feel linked to the Confederacy. In my life time the last Confederate Veteran, widow, and real son of a Confederate Veteran have passed on. I remember the last real son and have sat at a table across from him and his brother at a meeting of the Fincastle Rifles SCV camp #1326 where I joined on 28, November 1992. He was Calvin Crane and he lived to be 102. He earned 2 Bronze Stars for Valor in WWII. At his funeral on Sept. 21, 2019, he received full U.S. and C.S. Military Honors. Brother Judson wore my frock coat on the C.S. Honor Guard. Calvin's father was James Crane and he served in the Ringgold's Battery Co. B Va. Light Artillery. He came from Pittsylvania Co. Virginia where my home town Danville is located. Now the memory of the old south continues to live on in the new south.

Lynell Jones LeViner has had her ancestry traced back to King Edward I of England. A distant cousin is the late Queen Elizabeth II whose 19th great grandfather was also King Edward I. Lynell had an ancestor mortally wounded at 1st Manassas, named Joseph Hutcherson. She had two ancestors that were in 'Pickett's Charge' at Gettysburg Pa. who were Reuben Ricketts and Green Wade Jones. Also wounded at this battle was another soldier in her family named John Booth. Ellis West Jones and Elisha Oakes, also Confederate soldiers, did not survive the war. Elisha Jones, her Revolutionary War ancestor, was with George Washington at Valley Forge, Pa. She is married to Mark LeViner and the two live at Stuart, Virginia. Mark is a member of the Wharton-Stuart Sons of Confederate Veterans camp # 1832 Stuart, Va. by virtue of Samuel A. Dowless. He is also a member of the Colonel George Waller Chapter, Virginia State Society located in Martinsville, Va. of the National Society of the Sons of the American Revolution, by virtue of James Cain. Both of the ancestors upon which these organizations were joined are in the same family line.

Made in the USA
Middletown, DE
25 September 2023

39086991R00172